# *play winning*
# CRIBBAGE

### written, illustrated by
## DeLynn C. Colvert

**Copyright 1980 by DeLynn C. Colvert**

**Library of Congress Catalog Card Number: 80-67576**
**ISBN 0-9612548-0-7**

## 2nd Edition
## January 1993

Published by:
Starr Studios
P. O. Box 5604
Missoula, Montana 59806

# *Thanks...*

A very special thanks to my fellow cribbage players. Without their help this book could not have been written. The many pleasant hours playing cribbage with them will forever remain a fond memory.

A special thanks to my dear sister, Lorrie, for giving me my first cribbage board as a high school graduation present.

And, of course, a tip of my cap to the American Cribbage Congress for organizing the thousands of players nationwide into one big, happy, competitive family!

# Foreword

The game of cribbage has been around a long, long time and has changed very little along the way. The game is frustratingly simple on the surface, but can prove deceivingly complex upon analysis.

Ever since the game's invention in the early 1630's, a debate has raged concerning averages. In the early years a player of renown named Pasquin, declared the average for two deals was twenty-five points.

Later in the 17th Century, this average was calculated to be twenty-nine. Edmond Hoyle, *the* expert of card games, in the 18th Century debated this number by declaring that twenty-eight was more accurate for a two-deal average.

Old Ed Hoyle has commanded great respect the world over from card players, and to this day most cribbage experts agree that, indeed, either twenty-eight or twenty-nine is *the* two-deal average.

However, I have made a twenty-year analysis of these numbers, playing and charting thousands of hands. Contrary to old Ed Hoyle and other cribbage experts, I have found the two-deal average to be 26.4. Compared to a two-deal average of twenty-eight, this projects out to an astonishing 6.4 point difference in eight deals.

One present-day expert, basing his game on the twenty-eight-point average, projects the non-dealer of the first hand as the probable winner, winning with two points to spare, after counting first on the ninth deal of an average game.

Another contemporary expert predicts a twenty-nine-point two-deal average, with both players standing at 116 after eight average deals, making the game an end-game pegging toss-up.

But my analysis of the number of deals per game, and of who wins shows that **the dealer, not the non-dealer, wins the majority of nine-deal games.** This analysis is supported by projecting the 26.4 average through nine deals. The dealer, after nine average deals, stands at 121.8 and has won the game.

Using this new 26.4 average as a basis, a method of play slowly evolved...a method I call the "Twenty-Six Theory"...that clearly improved my winning average. Journeyman players that I had played for years at a 52-48 average fell at a 58-42 clip when I began using the "Twenty-Six Theory."

I joined the American Cribbage Congress and put my "Twenty-Six Theory" to a road test. I began competing in national tournaments. After some ten years of competition, this theory has performed very well, indeed, as I have won All-American honors (top ten players yearly) seven times, been crowned national champion twice (1986 and 1991), earned Master, Grand Master, and Life Master (the first ever!) ratings from the American Cribbage Congress...and was the 10th player inducted into the Cribbage Hall of Fame. Using the "Twenty-Six Theory" as a basis for tournament competition, my lifetime tournament average stands at .581.

This book presents a beginning player with the fundamentals, rules, and penalties, and slowly takes the player through the basic processes for improving their game. And, finally, the chapter "Cribbage for the Expert" describes the controversial "Twenty-Six Theory," which should make the journeyman player even better.

But most of all, I hope you will be rewarded with as many hours of pleasant companionship and competition with your fellow players as I have had.

# Contents

# Cribbidge?...No, Cribbage!

SIR JOHN SUCKLING 1609-1642
NODDY AND ONE-AND-THIRTY
POET AND PLAYWRITER
CARD PLAYER AND PLAYBOY
SOLDIER  AND POLITICIAN

# *Cribbidge?...No, Cribbage!*

"Her feet beneath her petticoat
Like little mice, stole in out
as if they feared the light,
But O, she dances such a way
No sun upon an Easter-Day
is half so fine a sight."

"Out upon it I have loved
Three whole days together;
And am like to love three more,
If it prove fair weather."

"Why so pale and wan, fond lover?"

These pleasant lyrics were penned by an Englishman in the early 1600's. Almost 400 years ago! Historians claim this Englishman is best remembered for his poetry...his plays...his literary work. But I wonder how many people have read them?

Historians must not be cribbage players. They must spend their lives in musty archives, never enjoying one of life's finer pleasures, wiling away a few moments playing cribbage.

The author of those lines is Sir John Suckling, and in total disagreement with historians, Sir John's most noted achievement is *not* his literary work. His most noted achievement *is* his invention of cribbage...that fascinating, exciting, fast-moving card game. Cribbage...that maddening, frustrating, simple card game. A game played by millions the world over, and after nearly 400 years, continues to grow in popularity.

NO! Sir John Suckling is not best known for his literary accomplishments! Without question, Sir John's fame rests with his creation of cribbage!

Ah, my lads, cribbage is the game
and no two games are the same
If you be willing
to wager a pound or a shilling
then sit down for a while
and I'll see that your smile
will fade with your ill-fate
when I cut this starter eight
for double pairs royal
'tis sure to make your blood boil
and then a fifteen-two, a fifteen-four
...are you asking for more?

*.the author*

## Sir John Suckling
### 1609 - 1642

Who was Sir John Suckling? He was born in England in 1609 into rather comfortable circumstances. His wealthy father was Secretary of State to King James I. Sir John, indeed, was born with a silver spoon in his mouth. *All card players should be so lucky!* His father died while Sir John was a child, and at the age of 18 he inherited a sizeable fortune, which he spent freely upon travel, women, and gambling. At 21 he was knighted by King Charles I. Sir John had a gift for words, and his poetry made him a favorite with the King and his Queen. *Actually it was Sir John's card playing ability behind the throne, into the wee hours, that made him a favorite. But he must have taken the King once too often, as Charles shipped him off to war.*

Sir John's military adventures were many. He served under the King of Sweden, Gustavous Adolphus, in Europe, and participated in many sieges...*out behind the back tents, taking all the raw recruits at "noddy" and "one-and thirty!"*

After the Battle of Leipzig in 1631, in which Gustavous won a brilliant but bloody victory, Sir John returned to England. He was young, rich, and handsome, and back in the King's graces. Sir John soon established a reputation for his wit and his poetry...and his skill at cards and bowling (according to historians he prized black eyes...or a lucky hit at bowls...above his literary achievements). In fact, his skill was such that he was the best card player and best bowler at court.

About this time he invented a new card game. A game he called "cribbidge." His new game was a variation of "noddy" and "one-and-thirty," both popular games at that time. Noddy consisted of markers (or counters), sometimes aided by a noddy board, counting in some fashion to 15 or 21. One-and thirty was similar, with the number 31 being the forerunner of the pegging target in cribbage. *Sir John invented cribbidge because he was having a terrible run of cards at noddy and was losing his shirt...and, perhaps, a new game would change his luck!*

At any rate, his wit, charm, card playing skill, and his fortune carried the day. Cribbidge caught on. It became a favorite among bowlers waiting their turn at the Bowling Green at Piccadilly. This fast-paced, fast-counting game was well suited to the short time between bowling matches.

But not everyone was taken with Sir John's new game. His sisters didn't relish it and reports describe how they came weeping to the Bowling Green to dissuade their brother from playing cribbidge. They feared he would lose their inheritance. *They needn't have worried. As long as he stayed sober, this was HIS game!*

This life of bowling, card playing, writing, and courting women continued until 1634, when, according to historians, another Sir John (Sir John Digby) gave him a severe beating for making a pass at his fiancee. Sir John began to "seek more serious society." *Actually, Sir John Suckling pegged double pairs royal twice in the same hand to nip Sir John Digby in the rubber game of a fiercely contested cribbidge match, cleaning out Digby's wallet. A hardwood cribbidge board will, indeed, administer a severe beating!*

In 1635, Sir John (Suckling) was forced to retire to his country estates after Parliament passed a proclamation banning absentee landlordism. Historians report that he thereafter concentrated on writing plays and poetry. *But we all know the true story. The lawmakers, sick and tired of being cleaned out by this sharpie, passed a law to get him out of town. We also know that Sir John didn't concentrate on his poetry, but proceeded to teach the locals this new game of cribbidge, at the expense of their loose change.*

Civil war between the Scots and the English in 1639 cut short his pleasant country life. Sir John, loyal to good King Charles, joined the fray, supplying 100 troopers on splendidly attired horses. This generous patriotic gesture impressed his peers. *Actually, the troops were in his indebtedness, thanks to cribbidge losses, and his winnings paid for the splendid outfittings.* But Sir John and his troops shared in the Earl of Holland's inglorious retreat before Duns. Poor Sir John was the butt of an amusing ballad, "On Sir John Suckling's Most Warlike Preparations for the Scottish War." *No doubt it was written by one of his many "sore losers."*

But notoriety, good or bad, pays off in politics, and Sir John was elected to Parliament in 1640. Politics proved to be Sir John's undoing, though, as he was implicated in a rescue attempt of Thomas Wentworth, a political prisoner, from the Tower of London. *Thomas was a favorite "pigeon" who kept Sir John in pin money.* The rescue plot was exposed, and Sir John quickly gathered what he could *(three decks of cards and a cribbidge board)* and fled to France.

Not much was heard from Sir John after that. Rumors had him traveling to Spain with a black-eyed beauty, but the love match didn't last long and he returned to France not long thereafter. *The black-eyed beauty could only speak Spanish, and Sir John was driven to distraction by all that "diez y cinco por dos, diez y cinco por cuatro y tres por la seis, siete, y ocho..."*

The last heard of poor Sir John Suckling is that he committed suicide by poisoning in 1642, after what meager funds he had managed to take to France ran out. *The truth of the matter is he had wagered his entire stake on a game of cribbidge. Sir John had the game well in hand, having the deal and the crib hand, needing two to make his 121. Sir John pegged only one! His opponent was 29 points from game, and held the five of clubs, the five of hearts, the five of diamonds, and the jack of SPADES! The starter WAS THE FIVE OF SPADES! The distraught Sir John promptly drained a vial of poison straightaway!*

Sir John Suckling left a legacy of many plays, poems, and other written works, but of all his accomplishments, his invention of cribbidge has had the most impact on mankind.

As with many words from merry olde England, spellings have changed, usually in simplifying, and Suckling's spelling of "cribbidge" has evolved into the modern "cribbage."

The game is played by millions the world over. It is especially popular in the United States and the provinces of Canada. And, of course, England continues to play the game with gusto. With cribbage's Anglo-Saxon origins, the game remains most popular wherever the English flag flew in the enormous English empire of the last three centuries (Australia, New Zealand, India, etc.).

Cribbage is enjoyed by people of all ages. This game --frustratingly simple, yet complex--has grown steadily in popularity. And after some 360 years, its continued growth attests to its sound design, and intriguing play.

A game can be joined almost any place two people can get together. Travelers find cribbage an excellent way to pass a long, monotonous trip. Aunts and uncles play with nephews and nieces, grandparents with grandchildren, fathers and mothers with sons and daughters. And in this book, you will be playing with Uncle Jake, "the snake."

Uncle Jake is a sharpie of my acquaintance, who would have given Sir John a run for his money. To learn to play cribbage like a pro you must play with a pro, and that's where "the snake" comes in. He'll show up when we get the cards out.

Today, as in Sir John's time, cribbage and gambling go hand in hand. Many cribbage players feel it's a waste of time if there isn't something on the game. Samuel Clemens--Mark Twain to most of us--wrote about this sentiment in "The 1,000,000 Pound Bank Note:"

> *After refreshments, tables were brought, and we all played cribbage, sixpence a game. The English never play any game for amusement. If they can't make something--or lose something, they don't care which--they won't play.*

No doubt about it, gambling adds a little zest to any game, whether for a few pennies or a few dollars. That's why cribbage tournaments abound in local clubs and bars where the stakes range from "a nickel a point" up to amounts that would have frightened Sir John's sisters.

But let's get back to the basics before we start wagering.

Sir John's game of "cribbidge" was played with five cards, with variations of the game evolving into a six-card game. Edmund Hoyle, the 18th century whist instructor who became famous for his book of game rules (*According to Hoyle*), had this to say about six-card cribbage:

> *This game is also played with the whole pack, but both in skill and scientific arrangement it is vastly inferior to that played with five cards. Still it is a pleasant resourse in a dull hour, and abounds with amusing points and combinations without taxing the mind much...*

Perhaps modern man has become lazy, or perhaps old Ed Hoyle didn't know as much as he thought he did, for six-card cribbage became the most popular, and now the six-card game is THE GAME!

Enough talk, let's get out the cribbage board and the cards!

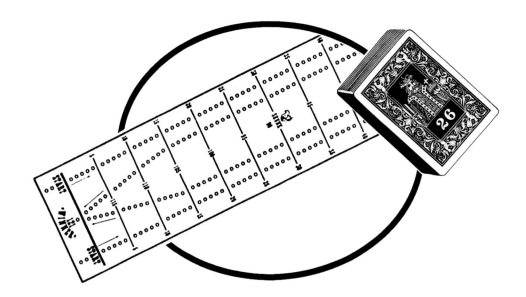

# Beginning Cribbage

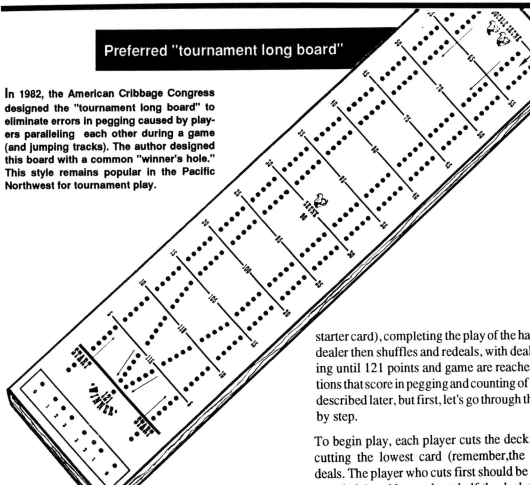

In 1982, the American Cribbage Congress designed the "tournament long board" to eliminate errors in pegging caused by players paralleling each other during a game (and jumping tracks). The author designed this board with a common "winner's hole." This style remains popular in the Pacific Northwest for tournament play.

How are points scored? First a dealer is established and six cards are dealt to each player. Both players discard two cards to form an extra hand called the "crib." This crib hand is the property of the dealer. After discarding, the deck is cut by the non-dealer and the top card of the cut deck is turned up. This is the "starter" card. Each hand is then played, with the non-dealer playing the first card. Play then alternates between players. Points scored (and pegged) with this interplay is called "pegging." After "pegging" is completed, the non-dealer counts his hand (in combination with the starter card) and marks his progress on the board with *his* pegs. *After* the non-dealer counts his hand, the dealer counts his hand (also in combination with the starter card), using *his* pegs to mark his progress. Finally, the dealer counts his crib hand (again in combination with the

starter card), completing the play of the hand. The non-dealer then shuffles and redeals, with dealing alternating until 121 points and game are reached. Combinations that score in pegging and counting of the hands are described later, but first, let's go through the game, step by step.

To begin play, each player cuts the deck. The player cutting the lowest card (remember, the ace is low) deals. The player who cuts first should be a gentleman (or a lady) and leave about half the deck for the other player to cut. Also, cribbage rules call for a cut at least four cards deep for the first cut, and at least four cards must be left on the second cut.

The player cutting the ace has won the deal

The dealer shuffles the cards (the non-dealer can demand to re-shuffle, but the dealer gets the last shuffle) and he deals six cards, one at a time, face down, alternating between players. Because cribbage is a "gentleman's" game, you may choose not to cut after the shuffle. In tournament cribbage, however, a cut by the non-dealer is *mandatory.* In a friendly game, the players can choose whether to cut or not.

The two players pick up their six cards. Each discards two cards face down to the "crib"...forming an extra hand to be counted and scored by the dealer (*after* the hands have been counted).

After the crib hand has been formed, the non-dealer cuts the deck. The dealer turns the top card of the cut deck face up. This card is called the "starter card." If the starter card is a jack, the dealer promptly announces "two for the jack" and pegs two points on the cribbage board.

Now we are ready to begin play, called "pegging." Remember, the cards are counted at face value (the ace is valued at one, the king at ten, etc.). First, let's identify the combinations of cards that score points in pegging:

## Scoring in Pegging

**Cutting the jack as the starter card: dealer scores two points.**

**Pair: two points.**

**Three of a kind (pairs royal): six points.**

**Four of a kind (double pairs royal): 12 points.**

**Run (or sequence): one point for each card in the run (minimum of three, maximum of five).**

**Running count totaling fifteen: two points.**

**"Go" (under thirty-one): one point.**

**"Thirty-one" (exactly): two points.**

In pegging, the non-dealer plays first, then the dealer, with play then alternating between them. Counting cards at their face value, the count continues to go higher with each card played. The object or target is "thirty-one." If thirty-one cannot be scored exactly, the player who played last gets a "go" and pegs one point. If he reaches thirty-one, he pegs two points. The count cannot exceed thirty-one. If a player is stymied and cannot play further, he announces "go." His opponent continues to play his cards, if possible. His goal is thirty-one. If he reaches it, he collects two points, if not he collects one point for the "go." Pegging resumes with the remaining cards in the hand and play alternates. If your opponent played the last card and received the "go," it is your turn to begin a new sequence to thirty-one.

Let's go through a few examples of pegging. The non-dealer begins play by choosing a card from his hand and laying it down in front of him face up and announcing its value. For example, if it is the four of diamonds, he announces "four" (suits are NOT announced in pegging). The dealer responds by laying down another four in front of himself (the dealer and non-dealer keep their hands separated) and says "eight, and two for the pair" and promptly pegs two points. The non-dealer continues play by laying a seven, saying "fifteen...two" (meaning the count is at fifteen and he pegs two points for the fifteen). The dealer plays a jack and says "twenty-five." The non-dealer follows with a five and exclaims "thirty." The dealer doesn't have an ace and says "go." The non-dealer, also without an ace, pegs his one point for the "go."

Now the dealer starts a new sequence to thirty-one. The dealer plays a king, announcing "ten;" the non-dealer follows with his last card, a jack, saying "twenty," and the dealer follows with his last card, luckily a queen, to form a run of three, and says "thirty, a run of three and one for last card" and pegs four holes.

Reviewing this hand, the non-dealer scored three points (two for the fifteen, one for the go). The dealer scored six points (two for the pair of fours, three for the run of the jack, queen, king, and one for last card).

For a diagram of this sequence, see top of next page.

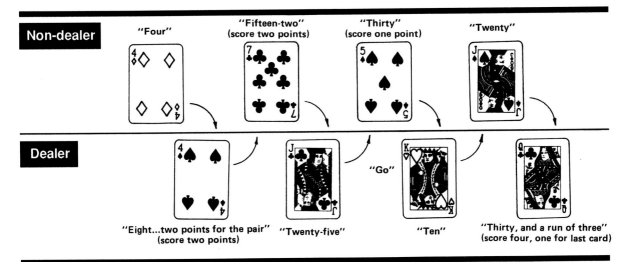

**Non-dealer**

"Four" — "Fifteen-two" (score two points) — "Thirty" (score one point) — "Twenty"

**Dealer**

"Eight...two points for the pair" (score two points) — "Twenty-five" — "Go" — "Ten" — "Thirty, and a run of three" (score four, one for last card)

*Let's peg a few hands to get the feel of the process:*

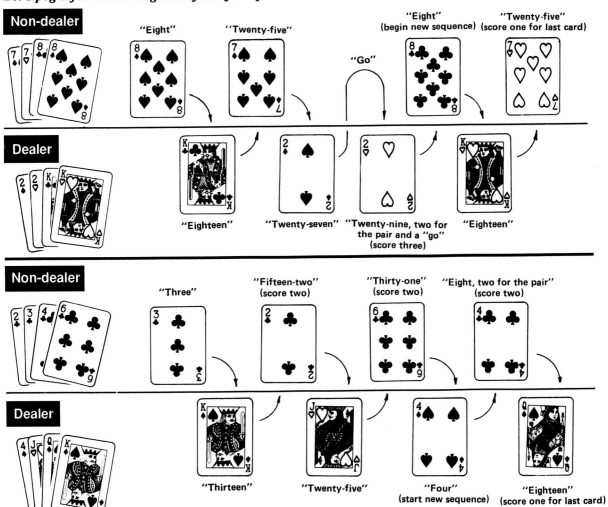

**Non-dealer**

"Eight" — "Twenty-five" — "Go" — "Eight" (begin new sequence) — "Twenty-five" (score one for last card)

**Dealer**

"Eighteen" — "Twenty-seven" — "Twenty-nine, two for the pair and a "go"" (score three) — "Eighteen"

**Non-dealer**

"Three" — "Fifteen-two" (score two) — "Thirty-one" (score two) — "Eight, two for the pair" (score two)

**Dealer**

"Thirteen" — "Twenty-five" — "Four" (start new sequence) — "Eighteen" (score one for last card)

The run in pegging is three (or more) cards that form a numerical run. They need *not* be played in order, but must form a sequence uninterrupted by any "foreign" card. Your opponent's card, combined with your cards, form runs. In a case of a "go," you may play out your remaining cards to form a run, and your opponent may do likewise. A run *cannot* be continued after thirty-one has been reached. One point is scored for each card in the run. A three-card run is three points, a four-card run is four points, and so on. The longest run possible in pegging is a seven-point run (ace-2-3-4-5-6-7). This peg count is 28, making the eight-card run impossible. Another ace could be played last to form another run of seven, however (ace-2-3-4-5-6-7-ace).

The key question when a run's legitimacy is in doubt is, "do the cards form a sequence, no matter what order played?" For example, the peg is as follows: 7, 9, 8 (score a run of three), then a 6 is added (score a run of four). The count is at thirty and is a go. No further cards can be played on this run. The count begins again. Another example: 5, 3, 2, 4 (score a run of four), ace (score a run of five and two points for the total peg score of fifteen...seven points in all), 6 (score a run of six). A run may be formed back to back with another run. An example: 4, 3, 5 (score a run of three), then a 4, using the previous two cards (3 and 5) to form another run scoring three points. Let's go through a few more examples:

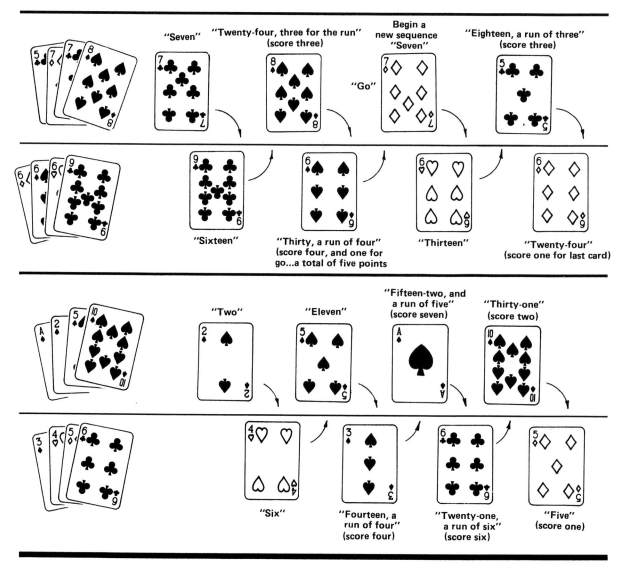

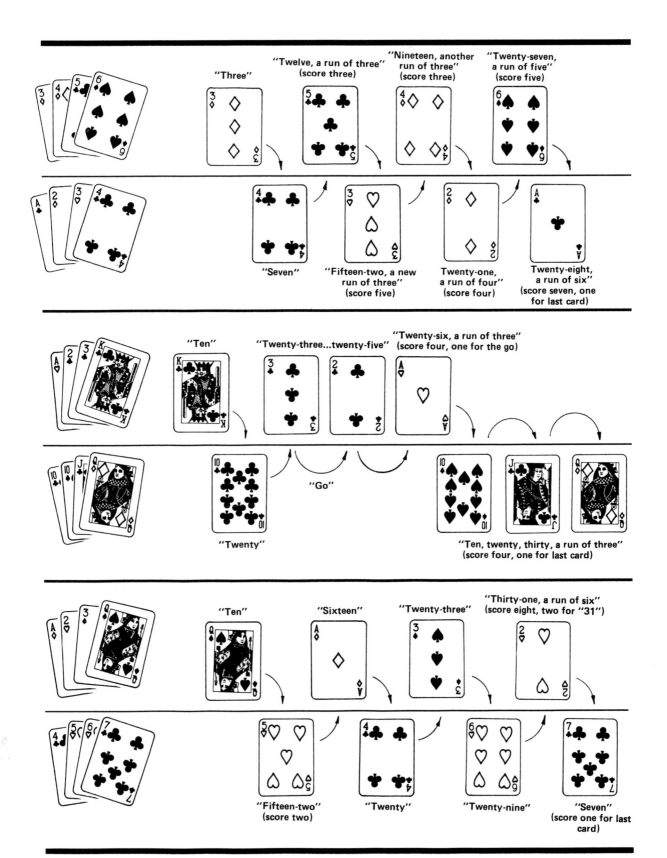

"Three"

"Twelve, a run of three"
(score three)

"Nineteen, another run of three"
(score three)

"Twenty-seven, a run of five"
(score five)

"Seven"

"Fifteen-two, a new run of three"
(score five)

"Twenty-one, a run of four"
(score four)

"Twenty-eight, a run of six"
(score seven, one for last card)

"Ten"

"Twenty-three...twenty-five"

"Twenty-six, a run of three"
(score four, one for the go)

"Twenty"

"Go"

"Ten, twenty, thirty, a run of three"
(score four, one for last card)

"Ten"

"Sixteen"

"Twenty-three"

"Thirty-one, a run of six"
(score eight, two for "31")

"Fifteen-two"
(score two)

"Twenty"

"Twenty-nine"

"Seven"
(score one for last card)

## Scoring the Hands and Crib

Pegging is completed when all eight cards of the two hands have been played. After pegging is completed, the hands and the crib are counted. The non-dealer counts his hand *first.*. This is the great equalizer in cribbage, as the dealer counts two hands (his hand and his crib) and would have a great advantage at the end of the game if both dealer and non-dealer counted simultaneously. If the non-dealer reaches "game" (121 points), the dealer *cannot* count his hand or the crib, and has lost the game.

Card combinations that score are basically the same as in pegging, except the starter card becomes a fifth card in the hands and the crib. In addition, flushes (cards of the same suit) now have value. Pairs count two; three-of-a-kind, is six; four-of-a-kind, twelve; runs (three or more) are valued at one for each card in the run. Cards totaling fifteen score two points. The jack, if it is the same suit as the starter card, is one point. Sir John named this special jack "Nobs." A flush (all four cards in the hand are the same suit) is worth four points. If the starter card is also the same suit, the flush bonus is worth five points. *The crib, however, cannot score a four-card flush. The crib must have all five cards of the same suit to count the five-point bonus.*

In addition, any run that has *different* card combinations may be counted.

This same rule applies to combinations that add to fifteen. Any *different* card combinations totaling fifteen score two points.

**Four of a kind: twelve points**

**Three-card run: three points**

**Four-card run: four points**

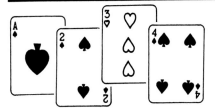

**Five-card run: five points**

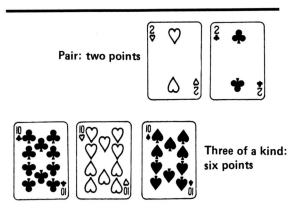

Pair: two points

Three of a kind: six points

**Any combination of fifteen: two points**

16

Jack same suit as starter card: one point

Four-card flush (hand only): four points
(starter card another suit)

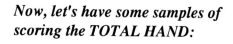

Five-card flush (hand and crib): five points

*Now, let's have some samples of
scoring the TOTAL HAND:*

Starter + hand

Fifteen-two's

 + = 2

 + = 2

 + = 2

 +  +  +  = 4

Single run of four

Nobs = 1

___

11

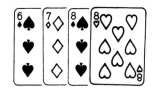

**A Double Run of three is** *always* **eight points,** *plus* **fifteen's, flushes, and Nobs** = **8**

## A Double Run

Fifteen-two $\quad$ **+** $\quad$ = **2**

Fifteen-two $\quad$ **+** $\quad$ = **2**

$\overline{\phantom{xx}12}$

**A Double Run of four is** *always* **ten points,** *plus* **fifteen's, flushes, and Nobs**

**10**
$\overline{\phantom{xx}10}$

 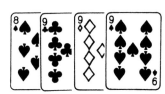

**A Triple Run is** *always* **fifteen points,** *plus* **fifteen's, flushes, and Nobs** = **15**

## A Triple Run

Fifteen-two $\quad$ **+** $\quad$ = **2**

$\overline{\phantom{xx}17}$

**A Quadruple Run is** *always* **sixteen points,** *plus* **fifteen's, flushes, and Nobs** = **16**

## A Quadruple Run

Nobs $\quad$  = **1**

$\overline{\phantom{xx}17}$

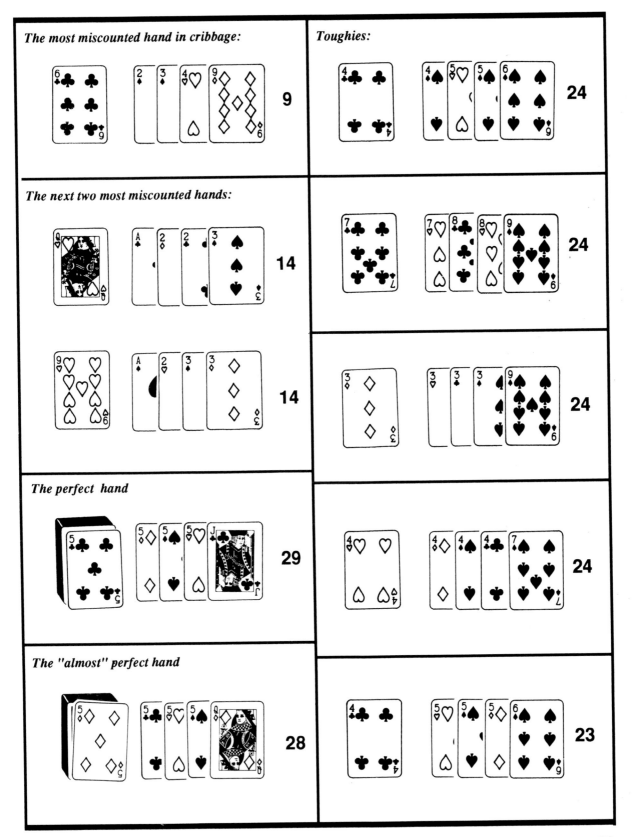

*The most miscounted hand in cribbage:*

9

*The next two most miscounted hands:*

14

14

*The perfect hand*

29

*The "almost" perfect hand*

28

*Toughies:*

24

24

24

24

23

19

After pegging and scoring of the hands and crib are completed, the deal alternates, and the non-dealer gathers the cards, shuffles, and deals a new hand...and he becomes the recipient of the crib hand. The deal alternates between players until the winner is declared...the first player to get his peg in the 121st hole.

Now you have the basic game. Uncle Jake, "the snake" (the villain in this plot) will beat you, the beginner, about 70 games out of 100. A beginner can win about three of ten simply because cribbage is similar to many card games, where luck in the deal plays a vital factor. But in poker, many a player is bluffed out of a winning hand. In cribbage, alas, even the poorest player will play his winning hand. And the expert must play every poor hand dealt to him. So, even the beginner will win his three games against "the snake"--the experienced player. And "the snake" is an experienced player. "The snake" is a pro!

Before going further, we must have some guidelines...some rules to follow. Rules to keep "the snake" in line.

20

# CRIBBAGE RULES

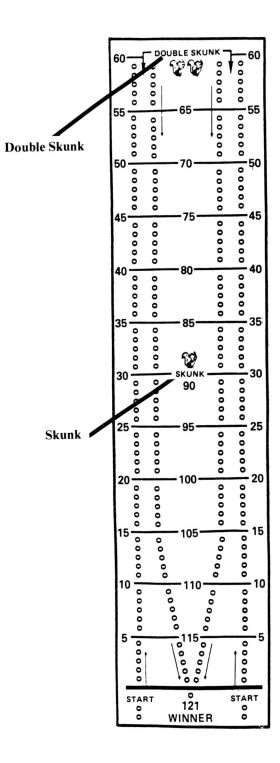

Double Skunk

Skunk

1  Before beginning a game, players must agree on:

- Whether the game will be 61 or 121 points.

- Whether a skunk (or lurch) will count a double game (in a 61 point game, scoring 30 points or less is a skunk; in a 121-point game, scoring 90 points or less is a skunk).

- Whether a double skunk (or double lurch) scores four games. This occurs in a 121-point game only. A player is double skunked if he scores 60 points or less.

- Whether "muggins" will be in effect. "Muggins" entitles a player to take for himself any points overlooked by his opponent (in pegging, hand, or crib). "Muggins" is declared after your opponent has removed his fingers from his peg, or when pegging, after he declares the count, and fails to call his points.

2  To establish the first dealer, each player cuts the deck. The low card wins the deal. In case of a tie, cut again. (Option: high card deals, if agreed beforehand.) The player who cuts first must cut at least four cards deep, leaving at least half the deck for the other player. The player who cuts last must leave at least four cards.

3  The non-dealer may shuffle the deck after the dealer shuffles, but the dealer has the right to the last shuffle.

4  The deck is not cut before dealing if agreed upon, but cutting by the non-dealer after the shuffle is mandatory in tournament play.

5  Cards are dealt one by one, starting with the non-dealer, and alternating between players until six are dealt to each player.

**6** Cards must not be touched until the deal is completed.

**7** The non-dealer discards two cards face down to the crib hand; then the dealer does likewise. The crib hand belongs to the dealer, to be counted at a later time.

**8** Cards once discarded to the crib cannot be picked up for reconsideration.

**9** The crib, once formed, may be touched only by the dealer, but only *after* counting his hand.

**10** The non-dealer cuts the deck for the starter card. He must cut at least four cards deep and leave a minimum of four cards. The dealer turns up the starter card.

**11** If the starter card is a jack, the dealer is entitled to two points, which must be pegged *before* he plays a card (the dealer can *still* claim his two points after the non-dealer has played his first card, however).

**12** The non-dealer *always* plays the first card in pegging.

**13** A card legally played in pegging cannot be recalled.

**14** If a card is *not legally played* in pegging, it can be recalled without penalty.

**15** After removing your fingers from the peg, the score cannot be changed (your opponent may claim "muggins" however, if you have agreed to that option.

**16** There is no penalty if a mistake is made in adding to thirty-one. However, the error must be corrected upon demand of the opponent before another card is played. Thereafter, the error cannot be corrected.

**17** Each player determines his count. No help can be asked for from his opponent or from spectators.

**18** The hands of both players and crib must be exposed to the opponent until he agrees to the count being claimed.

**19** Once the hand or crib has been counted and pegged, and the fingers removed from the peg, any unclaimed points are forfeited. In the case of a declared blank hand or crib, after the cards are picked up for a new deal, any unclaimed points are forfeited.

**20** Spectators shall not interfere in any way with the game.

# MISDEALING AND PENALTIES

Some irregularities incur no penalties. Other irregularities are penalized. These rules pertain to misdealing and *are not penalized:*

■ The dealer exposes one (or more) of *his* cards. The non-dealer has the option of calling for a new deal *if he has not looked at his own cards.*

■ The non-dealer exposes one (or more) of his cards. The dealer has the option of redealing, provided *he has not looked at his cards.*

■ The non-dealer is dealt *more* than six cards, but does not discover the error until *after* he picks up his cards: redeal.

■ The dealer discovers he has given himself more than six cards. The non-dealer has the option of drawing the excess card or cards from the hand and putting them on top of the deck, *or* the non-dealer may demand a new deal.

■ Either player is dealt fewer than six cards: redeal.

■ The cards are not dealt one at a time: redeal.

■ The deck contains a card or cards that are face up: redeal.

Some irregularities incur a penalty during play, including several for misdealing. These rules cover irregularities *that are penalized:*

■ After one card has been played in pegging, either player finds his opponent with an improper number of cards in his hand or crib: two-point penalty. Redeal. Option: either player adds card or cards from top of deck to short hand, or either player draws any extras from opponent's hand and places them on top of deck. Penalty remains two points.

■ Either player touches the deck before cutting for the starter card (after the deal has been completed and the deck placed aside): offending player forfeits two points.

■ Either player confuses his cards with the crib: two-point penalty.

■ If non-dealer looks at bottom card when cutting for starter card: two-point penalty.

■ A player announces "go" and neglects to play a card when he could count to thirty-one, or under: two-point penalty, and card that could have been played is dead (during pegging only).

■ Either player pegs more points than he is entitled: his opponent demands he correct the score and claims the number of over-scored points to his score as a penalty.

■ A player fails to peg entitled points: forfeiture of overlooked points *after* playing his next card.

■ When pegging entitled points, a player picks up his front peg. This peg now becomes his back peg, and the score is then recorded (his back peg is now his front peg).

■ Touching an opponent's peg: two-point penalty.

■ Touching your pegs without being entitled to score: two-point penalty.

■ A player removes his opponent's front peg: his opponent may claim a forfeited game.

## Beginning Play

Now you have the rules and the basic information to play the game. But how do you play the game? What is the strategy? How do you win consistently? No one wants to win only three of ten. Without basic strategy, playing each hand blindly, the beginner will be mired in a 30% rut. Old Uncle Jake will relentlessly win his 70%. If you are a beginner...and a wagering person (one of those Englishmen Samuel Clemens wrote about), you should not play a seasoned player for any loose change...unless you get 2 to 1 odds, and then only if you have won the first deal. Skill levels being equal, the first dealer will win about 12% more games than his opponent. Playing against a skilled player, this 12% edge, with a 2 to 1 bet, will make you a winner of the loose change. But no one wants to be given such an edge...it's bad for the ego! So on with learning the game!

## Recognizing Good Hands

First, a player must recognize what constitutes a good hand. Study the diagrams. They show the type of hands that pile up the score. Holding double runs that also combine into combinations of fifteens will make Uncle Jake sweat. For example, runs of 4, 5, 6 and 6, 7, 8 have combinations that add to fifteen. Also, runs of 7, 8, 9 do likewise. Ten-cards (ten, jack, queen, king) combined with the 5-card add to fifteen, and are easy to help with the starter card (the deck contains sixteen 10-cards and four 5-cards...roughly 40% of the deck). Also, small card combinations adding to five (ace + 4, 2 + 3) are easily helped by the sixteen 10-cards.

Recognizing good hands comes from practice. Learn to recognize which four cards of the six will score maximum count with the "right" starter card. Many times you will want to keep the very best count possible, regardless of the odds of cutting the starter card you need for maximum count, or, at times when you can ignore playing defense when discarding to your opponent's crib. Play a few hands at a leisurely pace and this knack of recognizing hands will come naturally. Secondly, study the rules. Many games are decided by a single point. An error, a missed count, or a single two-point penalty can be fatal. Especially so, if you have agreed to play "muggins."

## Examples of hand recognition (for maximum count):

Discard the 4-queen. A 2 starter card will score 14 points.

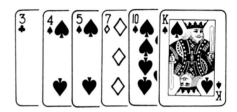

Discard the 10-king. A 3 starter card will score 14 points.

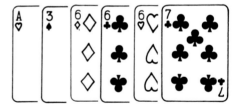

Discard the ace-7. A 3 starter card will score 20 points (and a 9 will score 18).

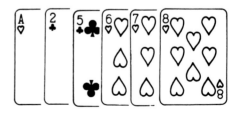

Discard the 2-5. Keep the flush. A 7 or 8 starter card will score 20 points.

Discard the 4 of diamonds and jack to your crib, the 4 of clubs and jack to Jake's crib. Any 10 card or 9 will score 12 points.

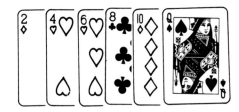

Discard the 2-8. A 5 starter card will score 9 points. However, the 2-4-6-8 combination is a better pegging hand...check the board.

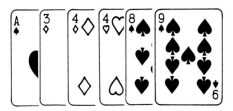

Discard the ace-9. A 2, 5, or 8 starter card will score 12 points. A 4 starter card will score 14 points.

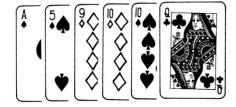

Discard the ace-9 if playing for absolute maximum. A jack or 5 starter card would score 16, however, the 5-9-10-10 combination would score 14 with a jack starter, and gives you the opportunity for a 12 hand with an 8 starter card. Check the board.

Discard the 9-10. The 5 of hearts starter card will score 23 points. Any 10 card will score 16 (the jack starter would score 20 points.

## Discarding to the Crib

After studying your six-card hand, the next question is: whose crib is it? If it's your crib, you want to lay away good cards...cards that will be the foundation (you hope) of a strong, high-counting crib hand. As Jake "the snake" would say when he deals, "I salted the crib, old buddy, look out!"

So if it's your crib, salt away. But do not destroy a good hand in the process. The bulk of your score will come from the hand, not the crib. It's much easier to draw one card...the starter card...to *four known cards* (your hand) than it is to draw to two known cards (your crib discard) and your opponent's *two unknown discards*. At times your hand will contain only two matching cards, with little hope of forming a good hand, regardless of the starter card. In this case, lay away the two matching cards in *your crib* in hopes of scoring at least a good crib hand.

Discard the 3-king. A 5 of spades starter card will score 13 points.

When the crib hand belongs to your opponent, your goal is to stymie the crib, to balk the crib...to make the crib as worthless as possible. Pairs, cards closely related that could form a run of three (or even four), cards that add to fifteen, and especially the 5-card, should not be discarded to your opponent's crib. Good discards to balk a crib are combinations such as a king-10, king-9, queen-8, ace-king, or other combinations that cannot possibly add to fifteen or make a three-card run.

The king is the very best discard to an opponent's crib, as the odds of it being used in a run are less than other cards (except the ace). The reason is because the king is the end card of the run, cutting the chance of its being used in a three-card run a full 33% over a queen, and 50% over the jack, 10, 9, 8, 7, 6, 5, 4, and 3.

To clarify these odds, the king combines with only the queen and jack to form a three-card run...eight cards. But the queen can combine with the king, jack, and 10 to form a three-card run...12 cards. The jack combines

with the king, queen, 10, and 9 to form a three-card run...16 cards. Sixteen cards also combine with the 10, 9, 8, 7, 6, 5, 4, and 3 to form three-card runs. Again, the ace is also the end card of the sequence of thirteen, allowing only eight cards to form the three-card run. The duece can be combined with twelve cards to form a three-card run. But the ace and duece are not as good to discard as the knig and queen because the ace and duece can be combined with any card in the deck to form fifteens. For example: ace+4+king, ace+6+8, ace+9+5, 2+3+jack, 2+6+7, and 2+8+5. In addition, the ace and duece are valuable cards in pegging, for forming runs, fifteens, and getting the "go."

There will be times--agonizing times--when a decision must be made whether you should destroy your hand to balk your opponent's crib. These decisions come with experience. Board position determines your decision in many of these tough situations. Later in the book, we'll analyze position and strategy, but let's get the basics first.

The king combines with four queens, four jacks.

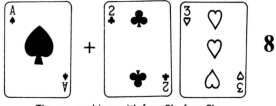

The ace combines with four 2's, four 3's.

The queen combines with four kings, four jacks, and four 10's.

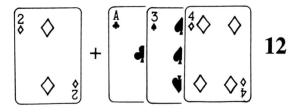

The 2 combines with four aces, four 3's, and four 4's.

The jack combines with four kings, four queens, four 10's, and four 9's.

The 3 combines with four aces, four 2's, four 4's, and four 5's.

In discarding to your opponent's crib, it is impossible to completely balk his crib. All you can do is *cut down* his odds of getting a good one. Any discard has the potential of at least 14 points. For example, you discard the king-9. Your opponent discards a pair of 5's, and the starter card is a 5--a 14-point crib! A longshot, but possible. Avoid discards that have a higher potential...especially those forming hands of 20 or more (7-8 or 4-6, for example).

In summary, when the crib is yours, discard cards that could be the foundation of a good hand...salt away good combinations. When the crib belongs to your opponent, discard dissimilar cards...balking cards! Study the diagrams for discarding to the crib. The basic process is simple, and with a little thought, you will quickly acquire good basic discarding ability.

Your crib: discard the 7-8
Jake's crib: discard the ace-queen

Your crib: discard the queens
Jake's crib: discard the 3-queen of clubs

## Discarding to the crib:

Your crib: discard the 9-10
Jake's crib: discard the 10-king

Your crib: discard the 8-9
Jake's crib: discard the 9-king

Your crib: discard the jack-queen
Jake's crib: discard the 10-queen

Your crib: discard the 3-king
Jake's crib: discard the 9-king

Your crib: discard the 2-10 (flush try)
Jake's crib: discard the 2-king

Your crib: discard the 7-8
Jake's crib: discard the 2-4

Your crib: discard the 8-10
Jake's crib: discard the 8-king

Your crib: discard the 5-10
Jake's crib: discard the 10-king of diamonds

## Pegging

Pegging! This is the fun part of cribbage! This is where the action is! The bantering, the faking, the psychological warfare...the thinking part of cribbage. Many a game is won or lost on a single bluff, a single misplay, a single gamble. About one-fifth of all points are scored by pegging. Give this aspect of the game some serious study. Until you master the art of pegging, your game will be mired in mediocrity. As Lord Kelvin would say, "Your knowledge will be of a meager and unsatisfactory kind."

The non-dealer *always* begins pegging by playing the first card. The dealer *always pegs at least one point.* The non-dealer *may* be held scoreless. These are the absolutes. From this basis, the sky's the limit. The peg may consist of only a single point being scored (by the dealer) up to the possibilities of scoring double pairs royal twice (four of a kind twice). You and your opponent both hold 7-7-5-5, for example. The 7's played first ("seven...fourteen...twenty-one...twenty-eight," "go"), then the 5's ("five...ten...fifteen...twenty...one for last card") could send the pegging scoring skyrocketing to 44 points!

Strategy becomes very important when pegging. Your board position in relation to your opponent is carefully weighed. Do you play offense ("play on") or do you play defense ("play off")? Are you far behind and must gamble to catch up? Is your opponent threatening to peg out and win the game? Do you desperately need a few pegs to win? These questions must be answered *before* the first card is played. A more detailed analysis of pegging is made later in the book, but for now, let's begin with basic strategy.

You are the non-dealer, and the game is fairly even. You want to maintain or achieve a superior position by pegging *more* than your opponent. This will be difficult. The dealer has the advantage in pegging, averaging about 1.4 more points than the non-dealer (the non-dealer averages 2.1 pegs vs. 3.5 pegs for the dealer). Before you make that first play, think ahead...if Uncle Jake pairs your first card (or 15's your card), how will you retaliate? Try not to let Jake get two free points. Have a card that will counter his two-point play. For example, you have a 4-5-6-7. Lead the 4, and if Jake pairs it, making the count "eight," counter with the 7 for "fifteen-two" and recoup your two points.

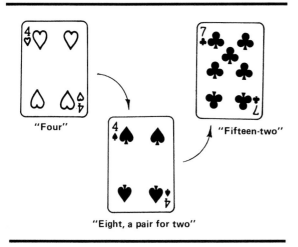

"Four"

"Eight, a pair for two"

"Fifteen-two"

The safest opening card is a card *below* the 5 (ace, 2, 3, or 4), because your opponent cannot make a "fifteen" for two points. And his odds of scoring are at least 57% less than if you lead a 5 (heaven forbid!) or higher card. For example, you lead from a single 4: the deck contains only three more 4's that can score...or three chances. If you lead from a single 9: the deck contains three more 9's *plus* four 6's that can score...seven chances. Or 57% more risk! And the 5 lead? Sixteen 10-cards plus three 5's...nineteen chances to score! This would be a mistake, to say the least (in rare cases, a 5 is the best lead...but we'll get into that later in the book). If you lead from a pair of 4's, or from three 4's, your lead is that much safer.

Train yourself to think in this manner. Count the cards that can beat you--the "losers"--and play the odds. ***Don't play hunches!*** Players who play hunches, or guess and ignore the odds, are losers. When in doubt, figure the odds. How many cards are out that will beat me this way...and how many cards will beat me that way? Don't forget your discards to the crib. And by all means, consider the starter card. There will be days on end that the long odds prevail, but hang in there. ***The Law of Averages is alive and well!***

Leading the four...

...three chances to score

Leading the nine...

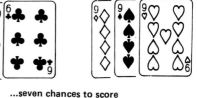

...seven chances to score

At times you will want to trade points ("play on") even if you come out on the short end of the score. This occurs primarily near the end of the game when a few extra points will allow you to peg out, or peg close enough to allow your hand (if you have first count) to score the 121st point and win the game. For example, you hold 3-5-6-7. "Playing on," you lead the 7, hoping to entice Jake into playing an 8 for "fifteen-two." If successful, you play your 6 for "twenty-one" and a desperately needed three points for the run of three. Jake may score an easy run of four with a 9 play, but the sacrifice is worth the much needed three points. When jockeying for position earlier in the game, the 3-card would be the safer lead from the 3-5-6-7 hand.

If you are the dealer, you will have the advantage of seeing the first card before making a play. Once again, think before you play. Jake, the non-dealer, leads a king, for example. Assume he has 10 and 5 cards to form 15's. If you are holding a 3-6-7-8, play the 8. If Jake plays the logical 10-card for "twenty-eight," you have the 3 for "thirty-one" and two points. Playing the 3 on Jake's king lead would be a bad play, since it would allow Jake to "fifteen" the play with any 2's he may be holding. Remember...count the losers. By playing the 8 on the king, the deck contains only three more 8's, but by playing the 3 on the king lead, the deck contains three more 3's and four dueces.

A common dilemma confronting the dealer is whether to pair the non-dealer's first lead. According to one cribbage expert, if a player pairs the lead, he will average .7 points on the plus side of the ledger. But other factors must be considered. If a player *always* pairs a lead, if possible, then his opponent will *always* lead from a pair, if possible. This cuts the .7 average profit down a bit.

Nevertheless, it is profitable to pair a lead, as a general rule. But look at the board position of both players. Can you risk a six-point peg? Do you *really* need the two points? Are you playing defense or offense? Do you have a safe defensive card, or are you trapped in a no-win situation? For example, Uncle Jake leads a 2. You hold a 2-3-4-4. You are playing defense. Your first impulse might be to play a 4, but pairing the lead and risking pairs royal (three of a kind) is the safest play. Remember, count the "losers." By pairing the 2 lead, leaves two losers (only two dueces remain in the deck).

But by playing a 4 leaves nine losers (two 4's. three 3's and four 9's). In this case, two losers vs. nine losers make playing the 4 a very poor choice (except if six pegs will surely beat you, but two or three pegs would not!) Of course, some decisions are based upon your opponent's habits. You must know your board position (and your opponent's board position). But, when in doubt, pair away!

The second card played by your opponent is the least risky to pair of the first three played. Of course, pairing the fourth card is no risk at all. The reason pairing the third card is riskier than the second is because many players try to trap your last card with a pair for a seven-point play, or simply keep a pair for last in the event their opponent is forced to play out his remaining cards after getting a "go" and the pair will then score an extra two points when played back to back. So, as a rule of thumb, *always* pair the second card *unless* a six-point peg will surely beat you. But keep a wary eye on Uncle Jake, who may get wise to your *consistent* style of play.

Study the diagrams on the next page for tips in pegging. With a little practice, you will get the feel for the numbers. You will soon learn to "dump the lone jack" (after the count is at twelve or above), not fall for the "sucker" plays, and *play the odds.*

*Play the odds!*

# Pegging Tips:

Lead the 7. If Jake pairs it, the ace will add to "fifteen." If Jake plays an 8 for "fifteen," your 9 will form a run of three (and if Jake has the 6 for a run of four and "thirty," your ace will recoup with a "thirty-one."

Again, lead the king. It is the least likely "ten" card held, and if Jake holds a 10, there is an excellent chance this will be his response, allowing you to pair it. The queen or jack lead would eliminate this chance.

Lead the king. The least likely "ten" card held by Jake will be a king. You do NOT want to entice a pair here.

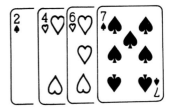

Lead the 4. If Jake pairs it, your 7 for "fifteen" recovers your two points. In addition, the 4 lead's response is often a 9. Your 2 will make "fifteen."

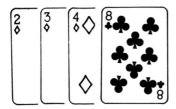

Lead the 3. This lead covers any "ten" card response, and forces Jake's 5 or 6's off the play. Leading the 2 covers any "ten" card responses also, but the 5 or 6 may respond instead of any "ten" cards that you are fishing for.

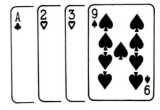

Lead the 3. If Jake pairs the lead, your 9 will counter for "fifteen."

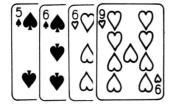

Lead the 6. If Jake pairs the 6 or plays a 9 for "fifteen," you have covered your play.

Lead the 4. It will draw Jake's 9. Your 2 will then make "fifteen." A king or queen response by Jake can also be safely paired by you.

31

**Jake leads a king**

Play the 8 for "eighteen." If Jake's logical second play is a "ten" card for "twenty-eight," your 3 scores "thirty-one."

**Jake leads a 2**

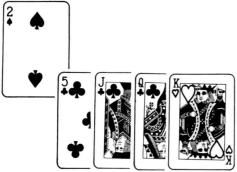

Play the 5 for "seven." You then have a chance to pair any jack, queen, or king that Jake may follow. The 5 would not allow Jake to play a 3 or 4 safely and would force any "ten" cards into the open.

**Jake leads an 8**

Pair the 8. You're trapped and the pair is the percentage play. Only two 8's are outstanding. If you play a 10, three 9's and two 10's can beat you (five cards vs. two cards...play the odds). However, if a six-peg will beat you, play the 10.

Now that you have learned the rules, know the basics of recognizing good hands, know the basics of discarding to the crib, and have learned a bit about pegging, well, Uncle Jake's winnings have suddenly shrunk dramatically. Now the best he can do is win about 62 out of 100. Now you can wager 2 to 1, even after having lost the cut for deal. But you still have a long way to go.

The game of cribbage, basically simple, has many nuances...nuances that can gain a point or lose a point. And for every point you can add to your side of the ledger means about a 4% gain in victories. If you can average just two points more than Uncle Jake in a 121-point game, you should win 54 out of 100 (an 8% edge). And that is the goal of this book...to make you the winner of 54 games against the expert! Sound insignificant? Remember, this is Uncle Jake! Against lesser players, your average will be much higher!

# Improving Your Game

## Improving Your Game

Let's go through the game once again, picking up every possible point, every possible slip by your opponent, every possible advantage!

Let's begin with the cut for deal. You are playing an average player and you feel your cribbage skill is as good or better than his. Neither one of you has an aversion to wagering on the game. You win first deal, then promptly say, "Hey, how about upping the wager? I feel lucky today." Actually, winning the cut for deal gives you a 12% advantage! The first dealer will win 56 of 100 games, on the average (with skill levels equal, of course). There will be days on end when even the dealer can't win, but the wager will pay off as surely as the law of averages exists.

Now that you have won the deal, thoroughly shuffle the cards, especially the bottom one. Having a knowledge of where any "extra" cards are--even one--can cost two points...or gain two points. When your opponent deals, keep your eyes on the deck. Careless shuffling by your opponent lets you see the queen of spades, for example. Your hand, after discarding, leaves you with the 10, jack, queen, and king. Naturally, you lead the safer card--the queen. Train yourself to remember any cards seen. A cardinal sin would be to forget what you discard to the crib.

Since you won the deal, your opponent cuts for the starter card. If he is careless, he may show you another card when he cuts the deck (and if he's a sharpie...he may sneak a peek at the bottom card of the deck he holds). Sneaking a peek at the bottom card of the deck is unethical (in fact, it's downright cheating), but in the heat of a rapid-paced game, it's extremely easy to sneak a peek. In tournament play, sneaking a peek at this card is a two-point penalty, and this penalty should be in effect for all games! In a friendly game, one warning should suffice! Insist that the top portion of the cut deck be held low and parallel to the playing surface. If you let your opponent get away with this practice, it could mean the difference between winning or losing a close game.

**Hold cut deck low and parallel to playing surface**

**Careless card handling**

If you feel you are a more experienced player, by all means play at the fastest pace possible and yet keep your game under control. This rapid play will cause your opponent to try to maintain pace, even though his game will suffer. His ego is at stake. Most players will try to keep up, even at the expense of their game. Conversely, if you are playing a better player, ignore his attempts at fast play. Keep your game *under control.* Play at you own pace. Think out your plays at your speed. Analyze the game thoroughly.

Another sly point: watch your opponent shuffle the cards. Anything less than a thorough shuffle could give you the needed edge when playing the hand. By remembering what was played the preceding hand, could swing a decision in the right direction. For example, three 7's were played in the preceding hand. Your opponent leads a 7...do you pair the 7 or play your king? If you don't deperately need the two points, it may be wise to lay off.

## Discarding Tips

Discarding to your crib, and to your opponent's crib is one of the key aspects of the game. Don't rush this decision. Thoroughly think out you play. If it's your crib, ask yourself these questions" Am I playing for maximum count? Am I defending Uncle Jake (he's near game and will probably need pegging points)? Will the cards I'm keeping be good pegging cards (cards that will shut out Uncle Jake's pegging attempts)? If it's Jake's crib, ask yourself: Do I need maximum count? Will the discards aid a potential high-scoring hand for Jake? Are they good defensive cards? Does your discard cut the odds of a good crib? DoI need to be concerned about Jake's crib? Think!

Study the "Discarding Tops" diagrams. These tips will add to your discarding ability and give you some insights as to the type of thinking that should accompany discarding.

As you continue playing, this skill will improve. The adage, "Practice makes perfect" is just as true in cribbage as in any endeavor requiring skill. Many of the tips illustrated will demand modification when your skill level increases to the "expert" class.

# DISCARDING TIPS

**Situation:**
2nd hand, Jake is black standing at 15. You are white standing at 11.

**Q: Am I playing offense or defense?**

**A: Offense. It's your crib, the game has just begun, and neither player has established a superior position.**

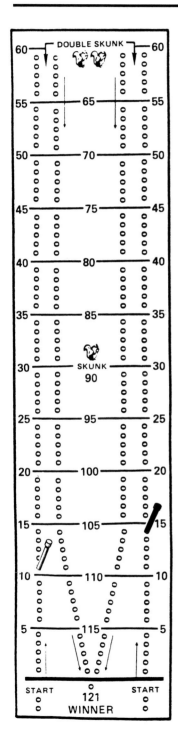

Discard the 2-king. The other alternative is the 2-10, but the king has the best chance of being discarded by Jake.

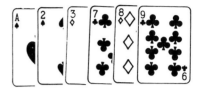

Discard the 7-8. Once again, any other discard would either weaken your hand or the crib. Make all your cards count, if possible.

Discard the ace-king. Many players make the mistake of keeping the run of four (ace-2-3-4), discarding the 8-king. The 8-king discards weakens the crib's chances of scoring--either the 8 or king is lost. With the ace-king discard, all cards have an excellent chance of scoring. If a 2-3-4 is cut for starter, the hand counts 12 (maximum)...and only 10 if the ace-2-3-4 is held.

Discard the 5-10. The chances of Jake discarding "ten" cards to your crib are very good. And the 2 works with your basic 6-7-8. Once again, the run of four does not always score maximum, as a 6-7-8 starter will score 14 (as will the 5 starter), but the 5-10 discard to your crib is preferable to the 2-10 discard.

Discard the queen-king. A 7-queen or king discard weakens the crib's chances of scoring. And if Jake leads a "ten" card? What an opportunity for a pegging bonanza!

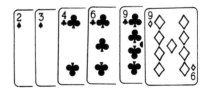

Discard the 6-9 of clubs. Since it's Jake's pegging lead, the 2-3-4-9 is superior to the 2-3-4-6. The 2-9 is a better offensive-defensive combination against the "ten" card lead than is the 2-6 combination.

# DISCARDING TIPS

**Situation:**
Jake is black standing at 53. You are white standing at 31. It is Jake's crib.

Q: Am I playing offense or defense?

A: Desperation offense.

Q: Do I need being concerned about balking Jake's crib?

A: Yes, but you must gamble to have any hope of winning the game. Play for maximum count.

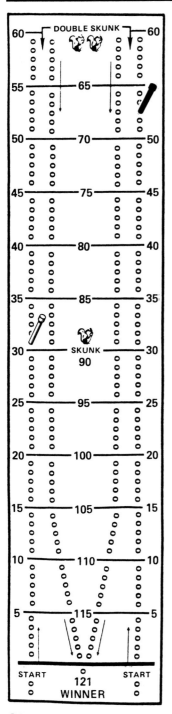

Discard the pair of aces. Then lead a 7. If Jake pairs your lead, the remaining ace scores fifteen-two. If you are lucky, the 7 lead may entice Jake's 8 (for fifteen-two), and you respond with your 8 for a "gambling" 23. With a break this may be a "go" and you score pairs royal for thirty-one (and 8 BIG pegs). And the ace-7-8-8 hand, with a 6 starter, will score a maximum 16 points.

Discard the 7-8. A 5-queen starter will score a maximum 16 points (seventeen with nobs). The odds are roughly 3-1 Jake will NOT match your 7-8 discard. Many beginning cribbage players play too conservatively and destroy a strong potential hand...especially in this situation.

Discard the 5-9. If you are fortunate and cut a 3 starter, you will score a maximum 14 points (a 2 starter will score 12).

Go for broke. Discard the 7-queen. The odds of cutting the 5 are 11 1/2 to 1, but, if successful, you're back in the game.

Discard the jack-king. The ace-ace-5-9 will score 12 points with an ace-5-9 starter (maximum for the hand). And by holding the lone 5, you have slightly reduced Jake's crib scoring chances.

Discard the 4-9. The 16 outstanding "ten" cards, if cut for the starter, give you an easy 12. A 3 starter will score 15 points. Ignore the heart flush.

38

# DISCARDING TIPS

**Situation:**

Jake is black standing at 115, needing 6 points to win the game. You are white standing at 114 points. It is your crib.

**Q: What are Jake's chances of scoring 6 points?**

**A:** Jake will score AT LEAST 6 points about 88% of the time when he is the non-dealer (study the charts in chapter five "What's the Odds?").

**Q: Is it possible to peg 7 points and win the game?**

**A:** Analyze the cards dealt to you and then decide.

**Q: If my cards DO NOT give me a chance to peg 7 points, how do I play the hand?**

**A:** Discard your hand to play maximum defense. Then play for that meager 12% chance you have to hold Jake to less than 6 points.

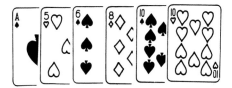

Discard the 10-10. Your best hope of winning the game: Jake must lead a 7 and you respond with your 8 for fifteen-two., then Jake plays his 9 for 24 (a run of 3). You respond with your 6 for thirty (a run of 4), and with luck, a "go" to win the game. Other pegging chances exist but your odds of scoring 7 points are severly limited, if Jake does NOT lead a 7.

Discard the 3-jack. Your chances of pegging 7 are slim. Play defense and hope for the best. Do NOT play your 5 on a "ten" lead. Play your 6.

Discard the 2-3. If Jake's hand consists of "ten" cards-5, you have an excellent chance to peg 7 points to win the game. This is an ideal pegging hand.

Discard the 10-king of spades. Keep your jacks for last in a desperation jack trap for 7 points. And keep the king of diamonds for a possible flush fake.

Discard the 10-jack. Your chances of pegging 7 are practically zero. Play defense and hope for thebest. The king is a better defensive card than the 10 or jack.

The basic combinations of the "Magic Eleven"

## *The Magic Eleven!*

Cards that total eleven are especially important in pegging. The 5-6, 7-4, 8-3, 9-2, and "ten-card"-ace combinations aid defensively and offensively in pegging. These eleven combinations are especially important when you need a strong defense. When Jake needs a couple of peg points to win the game, make every effort to keep a "Magic Eleven." The reasons are obvious. Sixteen "ten" cards (combined with 5's) are one of the most common hands held. And since 5's are rarely led in pegging, the "ten" cards are played first. The "Magic Eleven" easily scores thirty-one...shutting out Jake, and scoring for you. If you are playing desperation defense and don't have TWO cards totaling to eleven, try to keep THREE cards that total eleven. For example, 5-3-3, 9-ace-ace, 8-2-ace, 7-2-2, or 6-3-2. It's amazing how often this "eleven" defense works.

Even if defense is not of prime importance, when studying your six cards and an obvious discard is tough to figure, base your decision on the "Magic Eleven." Keep cards that total eleven. Your score in pegging will improve.

And your defense will improve! An example of a tough hand to discard: Ace-2-6-9-jack-king. Discard the jack and king instead of the 6-9. Even though the jack and king, combined with the ace, adds to eleven, the 9-2 combination is preferable. Since the "Magic Eleven" is especially designed to stop "ten" card leads, your jack and king, combined with the ace, are not nearly as effective as the 9-2. But if Jake plays a queen or king first, play your 9.

This is obvious if you think it out. A 9 played on a jack or 10 lead gives Jake the opportunity to score a three-card run. Playing the 2 on his lead gives Jake a chance for a "fifteen-two" play, but this is the least risky of the two alternatives. However, play your 9 on the queen or king lead as there is no risk of a three-card run.

40

Another example: ace-2-6-jack-queen-king (opponent's crib). Discard the 2-6, keeping the "eleven" combinations intact. And the odds for hitting the starter card for maximum count remains the same, whether you hold the ace or 2 with the jack-queen-king. Holding the ace, eight cards will give you a 9-point hand (4-4-4-4-5-5-5-5). Holding the 2, again, eight cards will give you a 9-point hand (3-3-3-3-5-5-5-5). Holding the ace will give you that little extra edge in pegging.

The 6-5 combination is the very best "eleven" to hold when playing defense...as this prevents Jake from "dumping" his 5 (from a "ten"-5 hand). For example, Jake plays a king, and you respond with a 6 for "sixteen." Jake simply cannot risk "dumping" a 5 for "twenty-one." However, if you were holding an 8-3 "eleven" combination...and played your 8 for "eighteen," Jake would probably "dump" his 5 at this point for "twenty-three." A lesser player would more than likely play up to your desired "twenty-eight" and then your 3 would make the thirty-one play.

The 6-5 combination is the best, followed by the 7-4, and then the 8-3 or 9-2 follow as the third best combinations.

A pegging tip at this point: do NOT play too rapidly on a "ten" lead, as a shrewd player will detect your planned trap! Hesitate a second or two, as if you are mulling over other combinations. I lost a very important game by playing from a 7-4 combination. My opponent played a queen...and I quickly slapped my 7 for "seventeen". He eyed me suspiciously, and dropped his 5 for "twenty-two." Alas, I did not have a 6, and lost the game, needing but two pegs to win. I am certain I would have won if I had hesitated before making the play!

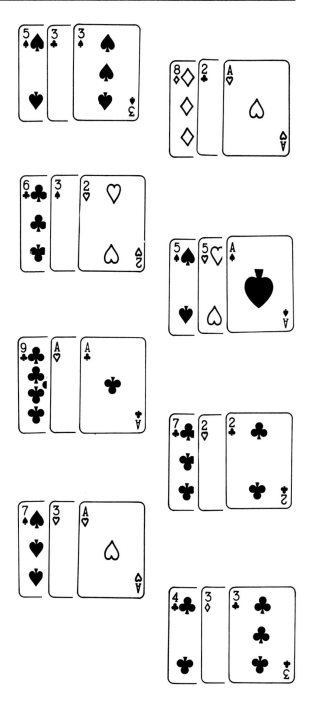

**Three-card combinations of the "Magic Eleven"**

# *Examples of playing the "Magic Eleven"*

**Your crib: discard the 2-king (defense); 2-6 (offense).**
**Jake's crib: discard the 2-king.**
**When playing defense, the 5-6 ("eleven") is the key, especially when it's your crib, and defensing Jake's possible "ten" card lead.**

**Your crib: discard the jack-king.**
**Jake's crib: discard the 9-king (defense), 7-9 (offense).**
**Holding the 2-2-7-9 gives you TWO "Magic Eleven's" (7-2-2 and 2-9).**

---

**Your crib: discard the 10-queen.**
**Jake's crib: discard the 8-queen. Lead the 3.**
**The "Magic Eleven" isn't quite as effective when you're the non-dealer and leading the first card (in this case, defensing Jake's crib is more important than keeping the 3-8).**

**Your crib: discard the queen-king.**
**Jake's crib: discard the 10-king.**
**The 3-3-5 will pay off two ways: a 4 cut will give you a 12 hand, the 3-3-5 is another "Magic Eleven."**

---

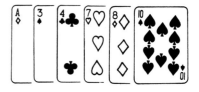

**Your crib: discard the queen-king.**
**Jake's crib: discard the 7-king.**
**The 2-2-7 covers the "Magic Eleven." And defense dictates the 7-king discard to Jake's crib.**

**Your crib: discard the jack-king.**
**Jake's crib: discard the 8-king. Lead the 9.**
**You have an excellent chance to peg 4 points with your aces ("thirty-thirty-one") if Jake holds a queen or a king. The ace-ace-9 covers the "eleven."**

---

**Your crib: discard the 10-king.**
**Jake's crib: again discard the 10-king.**
**The 4-7 ("eleven") will improve your pegging score. Your lead? Play the 4 and cover your play.**

**Your crib: discard the ace-10 (defense); 7-8 (offense).**
**Jake's crib: discard the ace-10.**
**The double "eleven's" (3-8, 4-7) will improve your pegging score.**

## The Pegging Traps

Setting traps in pegging can net tidy sums of points and can be the deciding factor in the game. The easiest card to trap is the 5, the next easiest to trap is the jack, then the ace, the 2, and then the 3.

## The Non-dealer 5-card Trap

First, let's trap the 5. The most common hand in cribbage is "ten" cards combined with one or more 5's. In fact, this hand will be played about one time in four. This hand offers several varieties of traps. Let's describe the hands you must hold if you're the non-dealer and playing the first pegging card. The slickest and easiest trap: your hand must contain three key cards, 6-6-4. Lead a 6. Jake cannot play his 5 (this would allow you to score an easy three-card run) and is forced to play a "ten" card. You play your other 6...and the trap is sprung! Jake must play a 5, making the count "27." You follow with your 4 for "31"...a run of three and two points for "31." A total of five points. Poor Jake comes up empty! This play works whether Jake has one or two 5's.

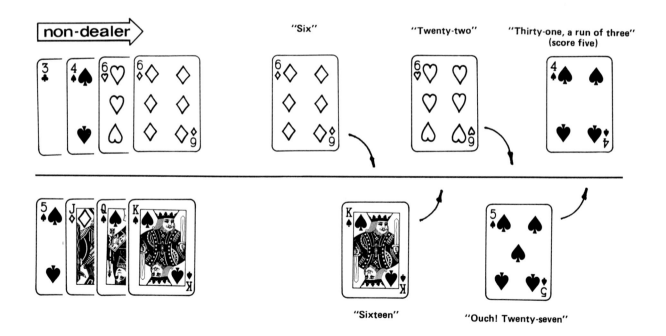

43

Another variation of the 5 trap: Uncle Jake must have two 5's to spring the trap so it is a little tougher to pull off. In this case, you must have four key cards: 6-7-7-"ten" (the second 7 could also be an 8 or 9). Lead the second 7 (or the 8 or 9), and almost certainly, Jake will respond with a safe "ten" card. You respond with your "sleeper ten" (if you're lucky, you'll get a pair for two points). If the trap works, this will be a "go." Jake is forced to lead his remaining "ten" card. You respond with your 7, forcing the trapped 5's into the open to run the count to "22." You then add your 6 for a run of three and a "go" for four.

Both traps usually net five points for you, and one point for Uncle Jake. A profit of four points pegging when you're the non-dealer is excellent, indeed.

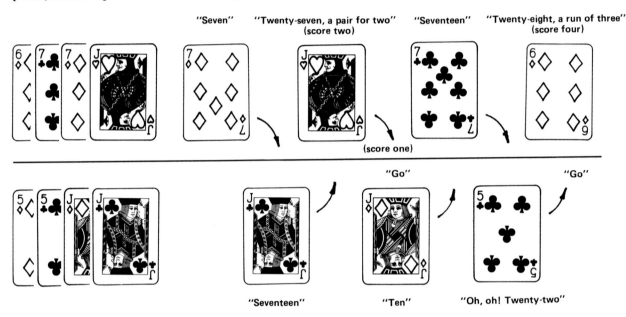

## *The Dealer 5-card Trap*

Trapping the 5 when you're the dealer: the key is at least two cards that combine with a 5 to form a run (3-4, 4-6, 6-7) and then pegging so that Jake cannot safely "dump" his 5 (or 5's) without risking retaliation of a pair or run. Let's go through one example of the dealer trapping a 5: you are the dealer and hold 3-6-7-8. Jake leads a king. Respond with your 8 for "18." Jake may "dump" his 5 here, but the odds are he will play a "ten" card trying for the "go" at the count of "28." You then play your 3 for "31." The trap is sprung. Unless Jake is a very shrewd player, he will probably lead his remaining "ten" at this point, and you follow with your 7 for "17." Jake's trapped 5 is played ("22") and you follow with your 6 for a run of three and a "go"...scoring four points. This trap nets five or six points, and results in Jake being blanked.

The trap has a good chance of succeeding if Jake has two 5's. But the odds are he will dump a 5 at the count of "18," and escape the trap. A player of lesser skill probably would not dump his 5 at this point, and would be trapped. The key to the trap is, of course, keeping the 3-4, 4-6, or in the example, the 6-7, for your last two cards to catch your opponent's 5.

This example also illustrates the advantage of keeping a "Magic Eleven." For example, your hand contains a 3-6-7-8-9-king. You are both within pegging range to win the game. Discard the 9-king (ordinarily a poor discard to your crib). The chance of a 5 trap, plus a pegging shutout (with the "eleven") make this the correct play.

A pegging tip: If your last two cards are a 5-"ten" and your opponent does *not* have a "ten" card on the table, and it is your lead, play the 5! You will escape any planned traps by your opponent! You will lead into a "15-2" at times, but this is preferable to a run of three (which will occur more often than the "15-2").

## Trapping the Jack

The second easiest card to trap is the jack. Regardless of who is the dealer, save a pair of jacks for last, and it will amaze you how often the trap works. If you have a jack-jack-queen-king, for example, lead the king. Most players will respond with the safer 5-card here, rather than pairing the king, risking a six-peg. If you lead one of your jacks, and Jake holds a 5-jack, the 5 is usually played, and the opportunity for trapping the jack is lost. The "ten" card lead will usually draw a 5 response. Keep your jacks for your last two cards to spring this trap.

On the other hand, if you have a *single* jack, "dump" it at the first safe opportunity (with the count "12" or higher). ***The lone jack is a liability.*** This is one of the most common errors that beginning, or even average, players make. Remember, "dump" the lone jack when the count is at least "12," making a retaliatory pairing impossible.

## *Other Traps*

Another excellent trap play occurs when Uncle Jake leads an 8 or 7, while you are holding the combination of 4-5-6. Entice a run with your 6. If Jake leads an 8, your 6 for "14" may entice his 7 for "21." Jake may be trapped! Add your 5 to the run for "26." A good chance exists that this will be a "go," and you add your 4 for a run of five! And a "go!" This combination results in Jake pegging three and with you pegging ten. A tidy profit, indeed! This is an especially good play if you're holding 4-5-6-6. If Jake decides to pair your first 6, you counter with pairs-royal. A no-lose situation. But don't employ this trap when playing defensively, as even a profit of seven points is worthless if it allows Jake to peg into range to win the game. Conversely, if you lead an 8 or 7, and Jake plays a 6, take a wary look at your hand. Do you have a 5 or 4 to cut off this "sucker" play? If you don't, think twice before creating the run for three. Check your board position carefully.

"Fourteen"

"Twenty-six, a
run of four"
(score four)

"Thirty, a run
of five"
(score six)

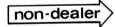

"Eight"

"Twenty-one, a run of three"
(score three)

"Ouch! Go"

Trapping low value cards--with the ace being the easiest to trap--is simply accomplished by running the count to "29" (if you're holding two aces) with one of the aces, hoping Jake has a lone ace for "30," then adding your last ace for "31" and a tidy eight points. With a pair of deuces, you run the count to "27" with the first duece. With 3's, run the count to "25" with the first 3. In all cases, the trap, if it works, nets a profit of six points. Five points if "31" is not reached exactly.

A variation is to run the count to "30" with the first of your two aces, hoping to pair yourself for a "free" four points. Running the count to "29" with the first of your two deuces, and to "28" with the first of your two 3's has the same result. But this play runs the risk of backfiring!

Uncle Jake may have the third ace, 2, or 3 and nail you. However, the odds are in your favor for a successful trap in all cases. You should give the trap a try *unless* your board position dictates otherwise.

The key to setting pegging traps is ***thinking ahead!*** After taking a look at Jake's first card, and the starter card, quickly make the best estimate possible of the logical hand that Jake is holding. Consider your hand, also, when making this estimate. After seeing Jake's second card, rethink your estimate. After seeing two cards, your estimate becomes much easier, and, of course, the third card will help that much more in predicting the fourth card. After making your best estimate of Jake's hand, set your traps! Keep thinking!

(Let's try to catch an ace) (Also faking a heart flush) (Eureka! It worked!)
"Eighteen"                "Twenty-nine"              "Thirty-one for eight!"

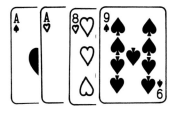

Situation: Your crib, and you need eight points to win the game. Jake has first count and needs only five points to win the game.

Jake

"Ten"

"Twenty-eight"

"Ouch! Thirty"

47

## "Sleeper" Cards

For every offense, there's a defense. Knowing that Jake will be analyzing *your hand* after taking a look at your first card, lead your "sleeper" card. A "sleeper" is a card that is a mismatch in a good cribbage hand. For example, in a 7-jack-queen-king hand, the 7 is a "sleeper." Lead the 7. Camouflage your hand as long as possible. Make Jake guess which side of a sequence your third or fourth card falls on. For example, you are holding a 10-10-jack-queen. Don't play the 10, then the queen, as the void between the 10 and queen makes the jack in your hand obvious. Play the jack. Jake may wrongly surmise you are holding a 9. Conversely, if you are holding a poor hand, by purposely leaving a void, Jake may wrongly surmise you're holding the card in the void. This deception makes your odds a little better of scoring on Jake's subsequent plays.

If you're playing offense (playing on) and want to pair as much as possible, lead from the **end** of a sequence of four cards. For example, the 9-10-jack-queen should begin with the 9 lead. A good possibility exists of a queen pair with the 9 lead, but quickly diminishes with the 10 lead, and practically disappears with the jack lead. In addition, this play cuts down on the possibility of Jake scoring the "31" followup if he happens to have a 6 for "15-2." You follow with the "dumped" jack for "25." Since a 6 has already been played, the odds are lessened for Jake to follow with another 6 for "31." In this case, Jake may be forced to play a 5 for "30" and a "go." This makes your following 10 lead that much safer. In this case, "dumping" the jack with your second card creates a 9-void-jack, but the lone jack is more of a liability than exposing a probable 10.

"Sleeper"

"Sleeper"

"Sleeper"

## Enticing the Play

Beware of the enticed play. If you lead a 4, for example, and Jake plays an 8, the odds are good he has a 3-card, enticing you to play a 3 for "15." He then counters with his 3 for a pair, recouping the two points. Or he has backed his play with another 8 (or a 6-7-9 to cover your possible 7 play). A good player will always attempt to play a card with another card backing his play. For example, Jake plays to "16" and your remaining cards are a 3-6-7. Play the 6 for "22." If Jake pairs the 6 for "28," the play is covered by the 3 for "31." Playing the 3 or 7 on the "16" would be "free" for Jake to pounce on. This style of play is critical to good cribbage. Think ahead! Try to get at least a trade when pegging. Give Jake nothing for free.

Of course, there will be times when your hand is in a hopeless bind and even Houdini couldn't save the day. Take your lumps and come back strong on the next hand. Be an optimist. A positive attitude (and playing the odds) is conducive to winning. A pessimistic attitude will put you in the loser's column. Study the examples of enticing the play. This skill is extremely important and must be mastered for you to become a winning player...a winning player against the "snake!"

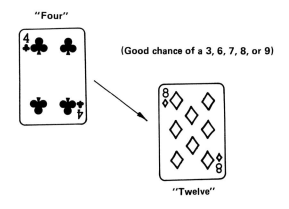

"Four"

(Good chance of a 3, 6, 7, 8, or 9)

"Twelve"

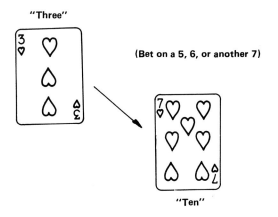

"Three"

(Bet on a 5, 6, or another 7)

"Ten"

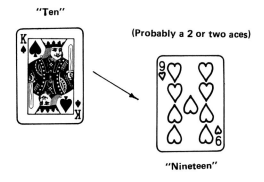

"Ten"

(Probably a 2 or two aces)

"Nineteen"

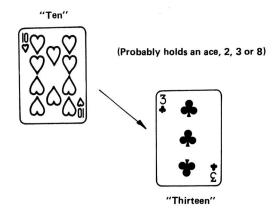

"Ten"

(Probably holds an ace, 2, 3 or 8)

"Thirteen"

## Playing the Flush

A flush is held about once in every six hands. On many occasions when pegging, a tough decision may be made by either "faking a flush" or playing your opponent for a flush (after seeing one or more of his cards). When discarding to the crib, whether yours or Jake's. keep the flush possibilities in mind. When you have the opportubity, place two cards of the same suit in *your crib,* and balk Jake's crib with cards of different suits. This is a very subtle point as you rarely cash in this play, nor does this defense rarely pay off in Jake's crib. But many times the discard can be made without affecting the count of the hand. Don't get careless and overlook the flush possibilities. Perhaps once in 100 games you'll collect five big points for a flush in the crib, and once in 100 games you'll stop a five-point bonus in Jake's crib by simply ***not getting careless!***

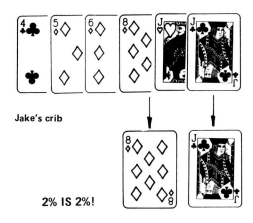

Jake's crib

2% IS 2%!

And there will be times whne you must break up a pair of jacks and give Jake a jack in his crib. Study your hand. Which jack is of the shorter suit? For example, you have a 4-5-6-8-jack-jack. You discard an 8 and a jack to Jake's crib. You have the jack of hearts and the jack of clubs. The jack of hearts is your only heart. The jack of clubs is matched by the 4 of clubs. Give Jake the jack of clubs. The deck (and Jake's hand) contains 12 more hearts and only eleven more clubs. This gives you a 1/46th (about 2%) better chance to cut a heart for the starter, giving you the point for nobs. How sweet it is when it pays off!

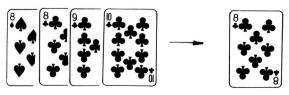

Lead the 8 of clubs keeping the
flush fake opportunity intact

Another subtle tip when pegging: fake a flush as long as you can (without making obvious boo-boos, of course). For example, you hold a 4-4-5-6 with the 4 of clubs, and the other 4-5-6 are hearts. Lead the 4 of hearts. You will be able to fake a flush if the opportunity arises. This play is wasted on most cribbage players, but when you move in tougher circles, every edge is analyzed. A good player will "take" a flush fake from time to time. Train yourself to make this play. Again, don't let discarding two cards of the same suit influence crib discarding selection, as the play is too subtle to pay off very often. Again, how sweet it is when it finally pays off!

Play the 3 of diamonds keeping
the flush fake opportunity intact

"Ten"

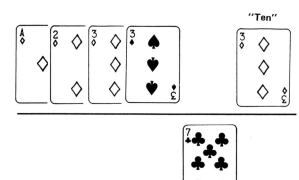

"Seven"

Check the diagrams to see how flushes influence play:

50

"Thirteen" (Fake a heart flush) "Twenty-nine"

(Play the queen of diamonds, Jake may have a flush) "Fourteen"

"Four"

"Twenty-three"

"Four"

"Ten" "Twenty-five"

(Jake may have a flush, play the 10 of hearts) "Ten"

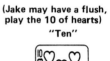

"Fifteen-two"

"Twenty-nine"

(Play the queen of spades instead of the king) "Seventeen"

"Twenty-nine"

(Normally the king would be played here) "Sixteen"

"Go"

"Seven"

"Twenty-seven"

"Six"

51

a "ten"...
or an Ace

## Logic

Logic! A five-letter word for *thinking!* After playing several hundred games of cribbage, standard plays become apparent. You will be able to develop "X-ray" vision, a la Superman, *if you work at it!* This is especially true when playing accomplished players like old Jake, the "snake." Beginning players make too many mistakes to allow full play of logic, but, of course, it works to some degree on all players.

A winning cribbage player must be able to "read" his opponent's hand rapidly. This ability is acquired through study, practice, and critical observation of your opponent's habits and style of play. Surprisingly, the better the player, the easier it is to apply logic to read his game...his cards.

Beginners play hunches, make unorthodox plays, and will surprise you with a poor play. These hunches and unorthodox plays, though confusing to the good player, will lead to the defeat for the beginner. And despite being able to "read" the good player's hand by applying logic, the good player will be tougher to defeat. The good player's game is based upon playing the odds, applying his analysis of your game, and his hard, cold logic...a very tough combination to beat. Without applying logic of your own, the consistent logical play from the good player will beat you. But, by applying good, sound logic, you will, at worst, play to a stalemate, and, at best, come out victorious.

Let's have an example of how to apply logic. Your analysis of Jake's board position indicates he will be playing defensively. As the non-dealer he leads a queen. Immediately, you may deduce he does not have the small five combinations (1-4, 2-3) or any 2's, 3's, or 4's, nor does he have a king (unless he has two or more queens). Why? A defensive play would be to lead a 2-3-4 (a 57% less chance of your opponent scoring on a small card lead--three losers vs. seven losers if a lone queen is led). Jake may have a lone ace, 5's, or he may have led a "sleeper" queen to his basic 6-7-8-9 combinations. But his lead, by logic, almost certainly ruled out any 2-3-4 cards remaining in his hand.

You play a 5 on the queen lead for "15-2." Jake plays a jack for "25." You now deduce Jake has all "ten" cards remaining, probably another queen and a 10, with a lone ace or king a possibility. Why? If he had two jacks, he would not "dump" one here, but would "dump" a lone jack or "ten" card (the most likely lone "ten" card to be dumped is the jack). If Jake does have two jacks, then he also has two queens (with the queen being the first play...the safer defensive play). And since Jake did *not* pair your 5, his chances of having a 5 have dimmed (unless he is playing desperation defense, and pairs royal would surely beat him). After seeing Jake's first two cards, logic decrees that the remaining two cards are, in order of probability, queen, 10, king, jack, and ace. Since the queen play was followed by a jack, the queen was not a "sleeper," but part of a basic "ten" card combination.

You play a 6 for "31." Jake begins a new sequence with another queen. Now logic tells you the odds are that the remaining card is most likely a 10 or king, the next most likely card would be a jack, then the ace...and then any "sleeper" cards (6-7-8-9) or a third queen. You would then play a card that Jake would *not* logically have in his hand--a 2, 3, or 4. You hold a 3 and a 4. You play the 3 for "13" (remember, logic decrees Jake may have an ace--if you played the 4 for "14," Jake may play an ace for "15-2).

Jake does have an ace for "14." You complete play with your 4 for "18" and a "go."

Applying logic has saved two points (not allowing Jake the last "15-2") and has not cost you, playing offensively, points.

Study the examples of applying logic. They are the ultimate key to playing winning cribbage!

## Applying Logic

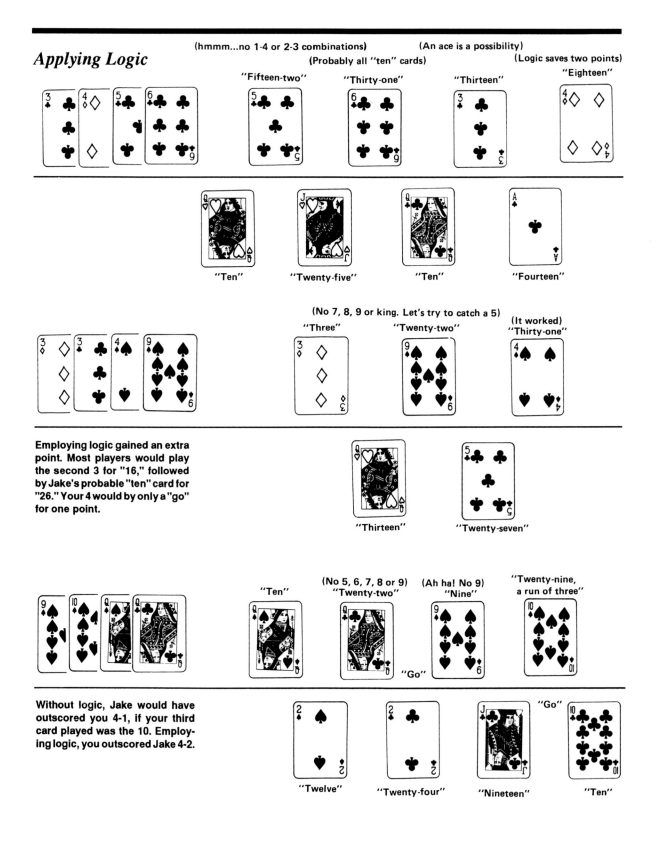

(Probably all "ten" cards)

(An ace is a possibility)

(Logic saves two points)

"Fifteen-two"   "Thirty-one"   "Thirteen"   "Eighteen"

"Ten"   "Twenty-five"   "Ten"   "Fourteen"

(No 7, 8, 9 or king. Let's try to catch a 5)
"Three"   "Twenty-two"   (It worked)
"Thirty-one"

Employing logic gained an extra point. Most players would play the second 3 for "16," followed by Jake's probable "ten" card for "26." Your 4 would by only a "go" for one point.

"Thirteen"   "Twenty-seven"

"Ten"   (No 5, 6, 7, 8 or 9)   (Ah ha! No 9)   "Twenty-nine,
"Twenty-two"   "Nine"   a run of three"

"Go"

Without logic, Jake would have outscored you 4-1, if your third card played was the 10. Employing logic, you outscored Jake 4-2.

"Go"
"Twelve"   "Twenty-four"   "Nineteen"   "Ten"

53

## Applying Logic

(hmmm, no 5)

"Ten"     "Twenty-six"     "Ten"

"Go"

Normally, the jack would be "dumped" on your second play. Logic saves a point. And since your 10 opening lead was "safe," your third card played is another "safe" 10.

"Seventeen"     "Thirty"

(No 4, let's try to entice a 5)     (It worked)

"Eleven"     "Eighteen"     "Twenty-nine, a run of four"     "Eleven"

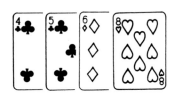

If you play your 6 for your second play, Jake would have paired it safely. The 4 as your second play is covered by your 5 or 6 if Jake establishes a run with a 2 or 5. Your use of logic and playing the "safe" 4 gives you the pegging edge of 6-3. Playing the 6 as your second play would have cut the margin to 3-2.

               "Go"

"Three"     "Fourteen"     "Twenty-three, a run of three"     "Six"

54

# The Percentage Play

Cribbage is a numbers game, and certain numbers combine with other numbers in a logical manner to form runs, the fifteens, and the pairs. These logical combinations can be played *offensively* and *defensively* to your best advantage if you study the odds and make the *percentage* play.

It's surprising how many players--even experienced players--misplay these common combinations. In most cases, these players have fallen into the trap of habitual play, and have ceased to *think.* And without thinking,

the percentage play slips away. Many times it slips away unnoticed. Other times the play is recognized too late and the "golden opportunity" is lost. And in many cases, this opportunity was simply missed because the *percentage play* was not recognized.

The following diagrams illustrate a few plays that are misplayed regularly by many players. Study the combinations, and play the percentage way, and your pegging score will certainly improve, both offensively and defensively.

## The Percentage Play

**The ace-4 (or ace-4-4)...lead the 4**

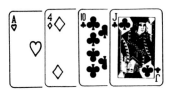 

**The 2-3 (or ace-2-3, 2-3-4)...lead the 3**

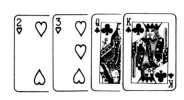 

Leading the 4 forces Jake's 5 or 6 off the play, increasing your odds of catching a "ten" card. Leading the ace allows Jake to safely play a 5-6-8-9.

The 3 lead forces Jake's 4-5-6 off the play. The 2 lead allows Jake to safely play a 5 or 6. You want to entice a "ten" card here.

**The 6-7-8-"ten"...lead the 8**

**Middle card combinations vs. a "ten" lead**

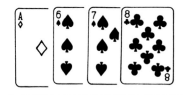 

The 8 lead keeps the 5-trap play intact. The king (or any "ten" card) would entice a 5 response (the very card you want to trap later). However, if Jake is playing desperation defense, lead the "sleeper" king.

The key to scoring with middle value cards vs. a "ten" lead is to keep combinations that combine with Jake's probable 5 for a trap attempt.

## The Percentage Play

**The ace-2-3-4...Jake's "ten" lead...play the 4**

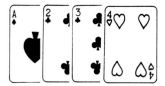  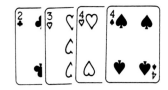 

When Jake leads a "ten" card, odds dictate he holds all "ten" cards with a 5 or 5's. Playing a 4 on his "ten" lead forces any possible 5's off the play and keeps your ace-2-3 run intact if Jake follows with another logical "ten" card for "24." Play your 3 for "27" for a likely "go." Then collect your run of three.

**Small combinations vs. a "ten" lead:**

The secret of scoring with the small-card combinations vs. the "ten" lead is holding your counters for last and running the count over "26" with your second play. In this example, if Jake plays a "ten" card for "23," you counter with a 4 for "27," setting up your probable pair of 4's for "31" and four points.

If your hand is a 2-2-3-4, your first card played would be the 4, then the 3. If your hand is a 2-3-3-4, your first card played is again the 4, then the 3 (the 2 would be "26"...a no-no!).

**The ace-2-3-"ten"...Jake's "ten" lead...play the ace**

Playing a 2 or 3 on a "ten" lead instead of the ace takes away your chances of scoring "31" if Jake has all "ten" cards. However, in playing *desperation offense* in this situation, play the jack on the 10. Your play is covered by a retaliation "31" if Jake plays a queen, or 9, for a run of three. Your ace or 2 will make "31" for two much needed points.

## The Percentage Play: the Four-Card Run

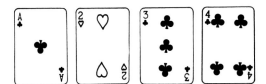

As a general rule do not hold this four-card run. Hold the ace-2-3 with a lone 9, 10, jack, queen or king if you need a 14-point hand. However, a 2-3-4 combination will escape Jake's "31" play if you are the non-dealer and making the first lead (with a 3) and Jake is holding "ten's"-5's. Also hold the 2-3-4 with a lone 6 or 8. A favorable starter card can result in a 14-point hand. In addition, keeping a "Magic Eleven" and a "sleeper" will improve your pegging score. Your lead? The 3 is the percentage play.

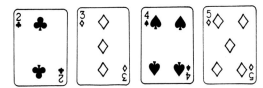

This four-card run must be played with discretion. If it's your crib, discarding a 5 with a "ten" card may be your percentage play. Jake's lead? Keep the four-card run, especially if you're playing offense. Keep the 3-4-5 in combination with a 7 or 8, however, as this hand will score 14 points with the right starter. Check the board before making your discard decision.

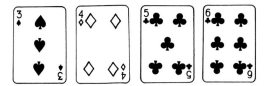

The 3-4-5-6 run is usually held as it can score 16 points (with a 6 starter). And with a 3-4-5 starter the hand will score 14. You must consider your discards if it's Jake's crib. For example, a 3-4-5-6-10-10 hand, the proper discard would be a 3-10 (Jake's crib). And if Jake will be playing defense, keep the 4-5-6-"ten" and lead the "ten." Your pegging chances are much improved with the 4-5-6-"ten" rather than the 3-4-5-6 (a tough hand to lead from when you are the non-dealer).

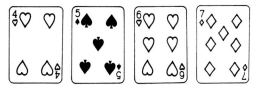

The 4-5-6-7 run is usually held as it also can score 16 points (with a 4 starter). But board position and discarding to Jake's crib may force the four-card run to be abandoned.

If it's your crib, break up this four-card run if you can discard the 5 with a "ten" card. The 6-7-8 held in combination with an ace or 2 is especially desirable. The 5 in your crib is the percentage play. Jake's crib? Hold the four-card run. Again, check the board and your discards.

The 6-7-8-9 is usually left intact. A helping starter card will score 16 points. Your lead? The 8 is the percentage play, keeping the 6-7 for a possible 5-trap. Also, if Jake pairs your 8 lead, you can escape with your 9. A 6 or 7 lead, if paired, puts you in a very bad position, with no "out" (or escape) card. And a 9 lead will likely draw a 6 for "15-2", leaving you with an untenable 7 or 8 response, or pairing the 6 for "21" (and an awkward, losing situation).

## *The Percentage Play: The Four-Card Run (con't.)*

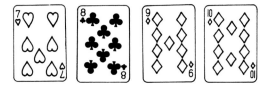

The 7-8-9-10 run is played with discretion. The 10 is discarded in many cases (for example, it's Jake's crib and you hold 2-7-8-9-10-king. Discard the 10-king). Hold the basic 7-8-9 in combinations with the "Magic Eleven" (2-9).

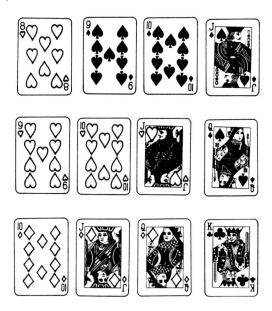

The percentage play for these combinations (if they are helped with a 5-6) is to discard the high end of the run to Jake's crib, and the low end of the run to your crib. Try to hold a "Magic Eleven" combination. Of course, if the remaining two cards do not help your hand, then hold the four-card run (example: 6-8-10-jack-queen-king, discard the 6-8). And as usual, board position plays a key role in making discarding decisions. You may want to discard defensively (8-king, for example).

---

Do I play "15-2" or pair for two?

"Three"

Do I pair the queen or play "15-2?"

"Thirteen"

The percentage play is "15-2." Jake probably holds "tens" and a 5 or 5's. By playing "15-2," Jake will probably play another "ten" card for "25." This will be a "go" and Jake will be forced to play a 5 if he has one. You then respond by leading your percentage queen. An excellent chance exists of a trap for a run of three. If you pair the queen on your second play, you stand the chance of having your jack (and 2) trapped. Think ahead. Avoid traps and play the percentage play!

58

## The End Game

More games are won and lost while pegging those last few points than by all the astute play of the previous hands. Most average games are decided by six points or less. (Study the analysis' in Chapter Six "What's the Odds?") Pegging becomes critical, to say the least, in these games. There are some keys to defensive and offensive pegging that should be basic to your game. Many of them have been covered earlier in the section on "Pegging Traps" and should be used in the end game when you're playing offensively...you need pegs to win!

### Defensive Pegging

But let's start with defensive pegging. Jake needs three pegs to win the game, and it's your lead (Jake's crib). You are dealt ace-4-4-6-7-king and need four points to win the game. Keep the 4-4-7-king. The "Magic Eleven" is covered with the 4-7 combination. You have kept a small pair (4-4) to lead from, giving Jake only two chances to pair your lead card. The king gives you a safe "out" card. If Jake plays a "ten-card" on your 4 lead, for "14," you play the safe king for "24." Jake's odds of scoring "31" with a 7 are cut 25% because you are holding one of the 7's. Of course, if Jake pairs the 4 lead, the game is over as you score pairs royal for six points and win the game.

This was an easy example. Many times you will not be dealt such ideal cards. The rule to remember in defensive pegging is to always *try to lead a card smaller than a 5, preferably from a pair*. "Dump" your lone jack at a safe opportunity, and always play the percentage play. Count the cards that can beat you and play accordingly. Don't play hunches!

The one exception to the percentage play: you have a lone 4 (or any lone small card) and were dealt a four-card combination of 6-9 or 7-8 (6-6-6-9, 6-6-9-9, 6-9-9-9, 7-7-7-8, 7-7-8-8, 7-8-8-8) leaving three cards to beat the 4 lead, and four cards to beat the 6, 7, 8, or 9 lead. Despite the one-card disadvantage of leading from the 6, 7, 8 or 9, this is the percentage play, as any good player (especially Jake) will keep all small cards dealt to him, knowing this will be your logical play...and the bias of holding small cards will out-weigh the one-card disadvantage.

If Jake is dealt an ace-2-3-4-7-king, the 7-king will be discarded. For this reason when counting your losers in a desperation defense, if a 6 or higher card is a loser by only one card...lead it! If the 6 or higher card will be beaten two more times? Don't do it! Lead the small card. The law of averages will bite you sooner or later playing hunches.

Another defensive tip: Jake needs four or more pegs to win the game. Don't get caught with one small card with the count above "21." You may be trapped into a run. Either dump a lone small card in the crib, or better yet, play it early in the peg sequence (usually the second card played) to avoid a trap. And if Jake needs five or more points from the peg to win the game, don't get trapped with a 4-5-6 as your last pegging card. Get rid of these potential losers. Especially the 5. If Jake needs seven or more points, the 5 held to the last card can indeed be deadly...being trapped into a 4-5-6 combination, or a 5-5-5.

Good defensive pegging comes from practice. Study your opponent; learn his habits. Does he always lead a 4 to a 9? Is he aggressive? Does he always hold a pair for last? Study his habits and it may be a game-saver in a tight spot. But once again, don't play hunches!

**Jake will attempt to keep these cards...**

**...when pegging will decide the game!**
**Nevertheless, an ace, 2, 3, or 4 is your percentage lead (see the probability chart on the next page)**

# Probability of Jake Scoring on Your First Card Played (Pegging is Critical)

*Jake will have these preferences when pegging is critical:*

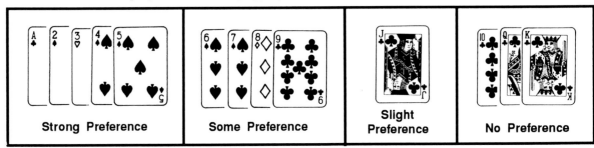

| Strong Preference | Some Preference | Slight Preference | No Preference |

What are the odds of Jake (dealer) scoring on your first pegging card played? Despite the strong preference for the ace, 2, 3, or 4, your odds in defensive pegging dictate your leading them, if possible (see chart).

## Pegging Odds

|  |  | PERCENT LOSER | |
| --- | --- | --- | --- |
| Of the six cards dealt to you *and* the starter card, you have seen: | Your first play | Pegging Critical | Pegging Not Critical |
| One 4 (or one ace, 2, or 3) | 4 (or ace, 2, 3) | 42%* | 28% |
| Two 4's (or two aces, 2's, 3's) | 4 (or ace, 2, 3) | 28% | 19% |
| Three 4's (or three aces, 2's, 3's) | 4 (or ace, 2, 3) | 14% | 9% |
| Four 4's (or four aces, 2's, 3's) | 4 (or ace, 2, 3) | 0% | 0% |
| One 6 or 9 | 6 or 9 | 65%** | 55%** |
| Two 6-9 combination (6-6, 6-9. 9-9) | 6 or 9 | 60% | 50% |
| Three 6-9 combination | 6 or 9 | 55% | 45% |
| Four 6-9 combination | 6 or 9 | 47% | 37% |
| Five 6-9 combination | 6 or 9 | 42% | 28% |
| Six 6-9 combination | 6 or 9 | 28% | 19% |
| Seven 6-9 combination | 6 or 9 | 0% | 0% |
| 7-8 combination odds same as 6-9 | 7 or 8 | Same as 6-9 | Same as 6-9 |
| One 10-jack-queen-king | 10-j-q-or k | 60% | 50% |
| Two 10-jack-queen-king-5 | 10-j-q-or k | 55%*** | 45% |
| Three 10-jack-queen-king-5 | 10-j-q-or k | 50% | 40% |
| Four 10-jack-queen-king-5 | 10-j-q-or k | 45% | 35% |
| Five 10-jack-queen-king-5 | 10-j-q-or k | 35% | 25% |
| Six 10-jack-queen-king-5 | 10-j-q-or k | 25% | 15% |
| Seven 10-jack-queen-king-5 | 10-j-q-or k | 10% | 5% |

*Formula (three 4's are outstanding among 45 unknown cards): $3/45 + 3/44 + 3/42 + 3/41 + 3/40 = 42\%$
**Empirical knowledge
***Assumes one 5 has been seen. Lower percent if 2 or more 5's have been seen

## Offensive Pegging

Offensive pegging: you need pegs to beat Jake, the "snake." This situation takes guile to beat the good player. Leading from a small pair may *not* be the effective lead. Even leading from a small card may not be the best lead. Entice the play; control the cards that Jake can play safely. Lead your "sleeper" card. Camouflage your hand. Work the traps. Keep two cards for last that will count for you (a pair or two cards that add to fifteen). If counters can't be held for last, keep two cards that could combine into a run (with luck).

Know your opponent's habits. If you know Jake plays a 9, if possible (and most players do), on 4 leads when you are playing desperation offense, and you have a 4 and a 9, then, of course, play the 4! And pair the 9!

If you need six or more pegging points to win the game, you need the luck of the deal. The best way to peg six or more is with a pair of small cards--aces or deuces preferably. Try to work a trap with the count past "21." For example, you are dealt ace-ace-8-9-jack-queen. Keep the ace-ace-8-9. You must hope for a "ten" card lead, and depending on whether you need four pegs or six, play your 9 (you need four pegs) or your 8 (you need six pegs). A good player like Jake will be extremely hard to trap, but an average player can be nailed from time to time. If you are not fortunate to be dealt a small pair in this situation, then concentrate on trapping your opponent into long runs, or keeping any pairs for your last two cards in a desperate try for a trap for pairs royal. Jacks work best for this trap.

Also, when six or more pegs are needed to win the game, try to keep a 4-5-6 combination for your last two cards (4-6, 4-5, 5-6) and hope for a run of three trap (and "15-2") with your last card for a nifty six pegs. What a shocker when you can pull it off!

Need 10 or more pegs? You must keep a pair of 7's or smaller for last for a desperate four of a kind on the peg. I have seen many, many players throw away their chances to win be leading from a small pair (7's or smaller) when their *only chance to win is to score four of a kind for 12 pegs. You must hold the pair for last for a chance to win.*

In offensive pegging, never lead a card that will cut off your chances to score. Example: You need three pegs and hold 8-9-10-jack. Never lead the 9 or 10. They cut your chances to peg dramatically. Leading the 9 forces all your winners off the play. But by leading from the end of this run you have a slight chance to score. You lead the 8...you may get a pair of jacks. Leading the jack, you may score on a pair of 8's. Keep your chances alive. Think!

Another example: you hold 2-6-7-king and need at least two pegs to win. The sleeper 2 is an excellent card to draw a 6 or 7 response.

And count the cards that will score for you. I lost a very important game needing but two points to win, holding 4-5-10-jack. I led the 4 and lost the game! I didn't count the winners before playing. Leading the 4 with my opponent playing desperation defense, gave me but six logical winners...three 10's and three jacks. The correct lead was the 10 (the 10 is held slightly less than the jack, and I did not want this lead paired!). The 10 could draw a 5 (three winners), but more likely an ace (four winners) or a 4 (three winners) for a total 10 likely winners. Leading the 4 gave me only six likely winners. A very bad play, indeed! My opponent did hold a 4 and would most likely have played it on my 10 lead for a winner! Don't play impulsively...count the winners. And don't play hunches. Control the peg with some old fashioned logic. Keep thinking!

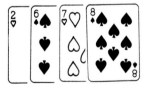 

**Jake will be playing defense...lead the sleeper 2**

**Jake has a defensive habit of playing a 9 on a 4 lead. If you entice a 9, your 2 will score a "15-2."**

# End Game Pegging

**Your lead (Jake's crib)**
**You both need three points to win the game**

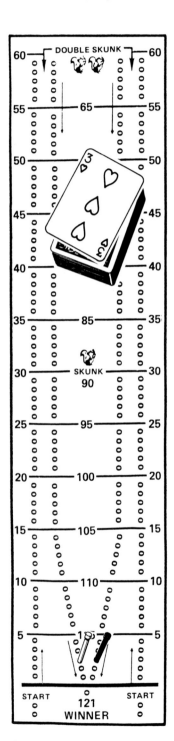

This is a subtle hand. Discard the 9-jack. Lead the 8 in an attempt to entice a 7 (53% chance). Your 6 then wins the game. Another option is to hold the 5-6-9-queen and lead the queen in hopes of enticing a 5 (and a 6 or 9 response is also likely). Enticing a 5 has only a 40% chance of succeeding--13% less than enticing a 7 (holding the 5-6-8-queen and leading the 8). And even if you were successful in enticing a 5, Jake would probably get the "go" and win the game.

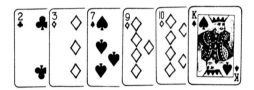

Discard the 10-king (this hand illustrates the unfavorable bias for "ten" cards when pegging is of prime importance). Lead the 3. Jake's chances of pairing the 3 are 27% (you have seen two 3's). And if Jake has a 3 for "6," your 9 will score "15-2."

Discard the queens. Lead the 7. If Jake pairs the 7, your ace will score "15-2." If Jake plays an 8 on your 7 lead, your 6 will form a run of three and the game is yours. The chances of Jake having a 7 or 8? 80% (less the slight bias shown these cards).

Discard the 7-king of clubs (you can fake a flush with the king of hearts). Lead the king of hearts in an attempt to entice a 5 (27% chance). If successful, pair Jake's 5 and hope to get the "go" and the game with your ace. The odds of Jake having the third 5? A meager 13%.

**Three of hearts is the starter card**
**Jake's lead (your crib)**
**You both need three points to win the game**

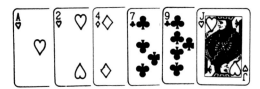

Discard the 7-jack. The ace-2-4 are key cards in this situation. You must peg at least three points. As the dealer you are assured at least one point. The 9 is held in preference to the 7 as it will run the count nearer 31, increasing your odds of scoring with your small cards. Of course, the 2-9 forms the "Magic Eleven" and will stop any "ten" leads. You will be forced to gamble and pair Jake's lead, if possible. The unbiased odds of Jake scoring pairs royal are 27%; however, Jake will be leading an extremely biased selection (if he has a pair, that will almost certainly be his lead). But the risk must be taken...pair away.

Ouch! This is a terrible pegging hand. Your best chances are of holding a pair for last, hoping to play them back to back for three points. Discard the 10-king. Normally you would keep cards to cover as many of Jake's as possible, but the "ten" card bias cuts the odds too low for pairing a 10 or king.

Discard the queen-king. Pair Jake's lead if possible. The 3 is your "safe" card (the 3 starter card cuts Jake's chances of having a 3). Entice any play that you can retaliate for two points.

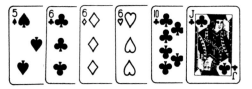

Discard two 6's. Play the 10 on any of Jake's logical ace-2-3-4 leads. If he responds with a "15-2," then play your jack. With luck that will be a "go" and your lone 6 will score "31." Then hope for a "ten" lead. And if Jake's first lead is a "ten," play your 5 for two points.

This is an ideal pegging hand. Discard the 8-jack. If Jake leads from small cards, play the 9. If he leads from middle cards, play the king. And if he leads a "ten" card (jack-queen-king), play the 9. If a 10 is led, play the king. Keep the aces for a back to back pair to win the game.

## Cribbage Psychology

We all know that people are creatures of habit. And cribbage players are no different. Old *Homo Sapiens* just keeps doing the same thing over and over. It's amazing how habitually we dress, eat, sleep, talk...it's just more comfortable to do "our thing" the same old way. Certainly, it's more exciting to do something new, but the facts are, we rarely do. And the older we are, the less apt we are to do something new.

The same is true of cribbage players. They get in a groove, a pattern. They consistently make the same plays, use the same mannerisms, the same voice inflections, and play at the same speed. Study your opponent. If you play Jake a hundred games, you should know what every little mannerism means, what typical cards are followed by another card. You should know if he is an agressive player, or a conservative player (incidentally, an agressive player will beat a conservative player by about 2%, skill levels being equal).

Some typical mannerisms that can predict a play or a situation are:

■ In a friendly game, Jake discards to the crib, (and despite the rules) takes a quick second look at his discards. More than likely it means that three of his remaining cards are of one suit and he wants to make sure he isn't discarding a flush opportunity. If he changes discards, play him for a flush; if he *doesn't* change discards, ignore a flush fake. Note: in tournament play, this situation will never occur, as it is a two-point penalty to look at your discards after they have been laid away...and a total NO-NO to change them.

■ You lead the first card and Jake takes a few extra seconds to respond (more than normal). The odds are he is debating whether to pair the lead or not. If he does NOT pair the lead, lay a trap for this card.

■ An average player has two cards left to play and hesitates slightly before playing. He is NOT leading from a pair. You can safely pair

his lead. Of course, this slip is seldom made by good players. In fact, if you are playing an exceptional player, look for the *reverse* to be the rule of thumb. *These sharpies will have developed a habit of hesitation when leading from a pair!* But, when playing an average player, continue to pair this "hesitation" lead until your opponent wises up to his mistake, and traps you with a "hesitation pitch" when leading from a pair! Conversely, many good players will give you the hesitation pitch ONLY when leading from a pair. The expert analyzes his opponent and chooses the method that works most consistently.

■ Your opponent has two cards remaining, and plays one without any apparent thought. This may be a careless play. The odds are good that your opponent is leading from a pair.

■ Your opponent runs the count to "27" with an ace. You have an ace and a 4-card but are unsure of taking the risk of pairing the ace (giving your opponent the chance of a pairs royal) or taking the "safe" "31" play with the 4. Hesitate for a second or two, faking a "go." In a fast game, your opponent may instinctively reach for his peg, giving away the fact that he does *not* have another ace (or any small card, for that matter). Then you can safely pair the ace, gaining an extra point. This play borders on being unethical, and as a tournament player, I do NOT employ this tactic...but, beware of players who will use this play on you!

■ You play an ace to make the count "27." You have no other small cards and you want to prevent Jake from pairing your ace. Fake another small card by *not* making a move for your pegs, *and* by subtly starting to pull another card from your hand. This could convince Jake you are holding another ace, and he'll play a safer card, saving you a point or two.

■ Some players carelessly let their emotions give their hands away. They bubble over with enthusiasm when they have good fortune, and pout glumly when they have a poor hand. Watch for any telltale mannerisms, especially immediately after turning up the starter card. It's amazing how poorly players mask their emotions.

■ Hesitations in discarding in end-game situations will give your opponent's hand away in many cases. For example, your opponent needs 8 points to win the game, and has first count. If he hesitates for an abnormal time before discarding, he probably has been dealt a poor hand...and you should peg accordingly. If he discards rapidly, he probably has enough to win the game with first count. You should then peg away to win if you have any possibility to do so. Once again, you must know your opponent's habits and mannerisms before recklessly pegging away.

■ Many good players will hesitate a second or two when they have two cards remaining in their hands, but only one will play. For example, your opponent is faced with a "27" count, and holds a 3 and a 5. If you catch him (after pegging has been completed) hesitating before playing the 3 (the 5 could not play), then this player will have given you a "warning" that you should enter in your "black book" (or your memory) for future consideration.

These are just a few of hundreds of possible mannerisms to look for. Study your opponent for every possible clue to his play. You'll be amazed what a creature or habit he or she is.

On the other hand, make every effort to keep your game from becoming too predictable. Play at the same speed as possible for all plays. At times you must take an extra second or two to make a tough decision. Try to duplicate this mannerism when you *don't* have a tough decision. From time to time, hesitate a bit (not too obvious, though, keep it subtle) when leading from a pair (especially when they are your last two cards). Remember, your speed of play can be a big clue to Jake. Keep your hand (and your emotions) camouflaged.

And speaking of camouflaging your hand with your mannerisms, keep your hand camouflaged *visually,* too! Some players get in the habit of arranging their cards high-to-low, left-to-right (or vice versa). A sharp player will pick this up. If, for example, you arrange your cards with the high cards to the left, and you play a 7, pulling it from the first spot on the right, old Jake will know you don't have any cards smaller than a 7. A top-ranked mid-western player has sharpened his skill at analyzing his opponent's card arranging...and this extra advantage has helped him in winning one national championship, and has aided him in consistently winning honors in tournament play...and is completely within the rules. Be careful, don't develop habits that will give your hand away! Get in the habit of mixing your arrangment of cards in your hand.

Ah ha! Nothing smaller than a 7!

You've seen a good poker player in action. Notice how he squeezes his cards for a look-see, and holds them in the palm of his hands so that opposing players cannot see his cards. That's not bad advice for cribbage players, too. This is especially true when playing a stranger in a tournament. He may be a sharpie, the cards may be marked, or he may pick up a mannerism in the way you arrange your cards. One less clue, the better. However, in tournament play, DO NOT slow play down with too many "tricks." Be polite and play at the same pace as your fellow players!

Speaking of marked cards, the danger always exists of your opponent cheating. The less said of this the better, since cribbage is a sporting game and has no room for cheaters. However, the ugly truth is a few players cheat. Watch for marked cards, short decks (fewer than 52 cards), crimped cards, "shiners" (reflective surfaced items), kibitzers who may give signals, dealing from the bottom of the deck, or "sneaking a peek" at the bottom card, or the bottom of the cut deck when cutting for the starter card. These tricks are performed by the "pros." However, even an average player may get into the habit of fudging a peg or two when you have entered a mesmerized state of mind after a long, grueling session of play. Other common tricks are double pegging when you are not alert, purposely miscounting hands or crib, switching cribs to gain an advantage, and purposely miscounting when pegging to gain an advantage. Be alert! 99.9% of cribbage players are wonderful, honest people, but, unfortunately, a few exist that will take advantage!

If you suspect cheating by manipulating the deck, the rules give you (the non-dealer) an opportunity to re-shuffle after the dealer shuffles. However, the dealer has the right to the last shuffle. This will make it tougher to manipulate the deck, but makes for an extremely awkward game. The best solution is simply not play with a suspected cheater, if possible. And, of course, always check to see if the pegging is accurate. Even an honest player will make a mistake in pegging...and it's amazing how often it's in his favor. If this happens too often, insist on the "muggins" rule, and this form of cheating will suddenly come to an end!

In tournament play, even if you believe your opponent to be a completely reputable player, and an error has occurred in his favor, and the rules call for a penalty, I feel it should be taken. He will be more careful in the future, and you are protecting yourself, and other players, if, by chance, the error was intentional.

# Turkey Plays

Gobble . . .

Gobble

Gooble

Some standard plays in cribbage occur rather consistently, and are misplayed by many players. Some are BIG turkey plays (rather obvious to a good player) and some are LITTLE turkey plays...mistakes that aren't too obvious and are misplayed by good players, too. Study the diagrams. There will be some arguments, or disagreements, with the LITTLE turkey plays...but that's what cribbage is all about. A friendly, fast-paced game with millions of options! Perhaps you can come up with better solutions. Most of these turkey plays have been analyzed through thousands of hands and are based upon empirical knowledge...and the school of hard knocks! What may work 49 times will lose 51 times...and it takes years of experience to know which plays work the most often.

## BIG TURKEY PLAYS

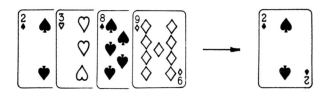

The 2 lead is a "turkey" play for two reasons. First, the play is not covered if Jake pairs the 2. Second, it probably will not draw a desired "ten" card response. The 3 is the play. The 9 backs the play for a "15-2" if Jake pairs the 3 lead. The 3 will be answered with a "ten" card more often than will a 2 lead.

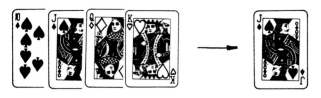

Double gobble, gobble! A jack is the most likely "ten" card held by Jake. And you have no card covering your play. Either lead the king (preferred) or the 10. Keep your jack-queen for last in hopes of forming a 3-card run. And if the jack lead is paired, you have trapped yourself.

Another bone-head play. If Jake plays a logical 6 on the 9 lead, you're in big trouble. The correct play is leading from strength...one of your 8's. Your play is then covered and you remain in the driver's seat!

Again, the 9 lead is not backed by a retaliatory card. Play the 10 and the odds are you'll trade points. Your third card should then be the 9, not the jack (if Jake played a 5 on the 10 lead).

Leading a lone 9 to a lone 6 is a no-no. If Jake plays a 6 for "15-2" and you retaliate with your 6 for "21," the possibility exists of Jake having a third 6 for pairs royal. Lead the lone 6 to the lone 9.

Pairing Jake's queen instead of playing a 5 for "15-2" could cost you a bundle of peg points. If Jake has a 5, and paired your first 5, the chances are excellent for your scoring pairs royal and a following "31" with the 6.

Leading the 2 is a turkey play for two reasons. First, the play is not covered in the event Jake pairs it, and second, the 2 will not entice a 9 as readily as the 4. The 4 is the correct lead. The 4 is backed by the 7 if Jake pairs it. If Jake responds with the logical 9, your 2 scores a "15-2." However, if Jake is playing desperation defense (end-game pegging, etc.), the 2 is a good lead.

# BIG TURKEY PLAYS

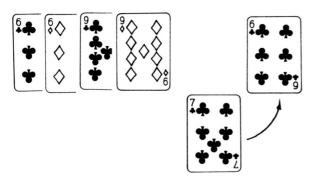

Playing the 6 on Jake's 7 lead gives Jake a chance at a free run of three with a retaliatory 5. Playing a 9 on the 7 gives Jake no better than a trade of points if he scores with another 9 for a pair (your 6 follows for "31"). If Jake decides to form a run of three with an 8, your 6 follows for a run of four and a probable "go" and a profit of two points.

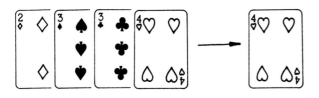

Leading the lone 4 is a gross mistake. It covers only Jake's 2, 3, 5, 8 and 9. The correct lead is the 3. It covers the ace, 2, 3, 4, 5, 8, 9, 10, jack, queen, and king.

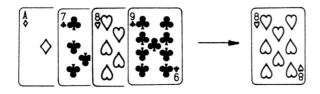

Oops! If Jake pairs the 8 lead you cannot recoup your two points. Lead the 7 and if Jake pairs it, your ace recovers the two points with a "15-2."

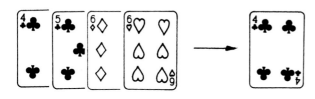

Unless you are playing desperation defense, this is a big turkey play. You have let a possible 5-trap escape. By leading one of your 6's, you may pick up an easy "31 for 5" (6-k-6-5-4 pegging sequence). The 4 lead will probably draw a "10" card, and you come with a single "go" at best.

# LITTLE TURKEY PLAYS

Little turkey plays . These subtle plays are the fine line between winning and losing with experienced players. These plays, if consistently played against the odds, will slowly eat you alive. In tournament play, with many qualifying round games determining if you qualify for the playoffs (and the prize money), these subtle plays can cost a game or two...and your chances of winning will have escaped. One two-point slipup can be the difference between winning the championship...or going home a loser!

The 3 is the correct lead, but the flush fake opportunity has escaped. Lead the 3 of spades.

The king is a poor lead. A slim hope of pairing a 10 exists with the king lead, but leading the 2 (the correct card) gives you the chance of pairing a 10-queen-king (three cards vs. the one card opportunity the king lead offers.

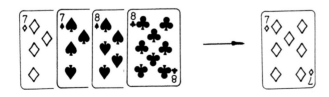

Oops. Leading the 7 will give Jake that slim opportunity for double pairs royal (if he also has a pair of 7's). Leading an 8 takes away that chance.

# LITTLE TURKEY PLAYS

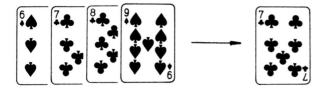

This is one of the most common mistakes cribbage players make. Leading the 7 allows the 5-trap to escape, and, in addition, allows "ten"-5 combinations to get the "go." The correct lead is the 8, keeping a 5-trap try intact and if Jake plays a following "ten" card, the 9 runs the count to "27," getting the "go" if Jake has a 5 (and no smaller cards).

Playing offensively, the queen is a poor lead, as it forces the 10-jack-king off the play, minimizing your chances of scoring three or four points with your aces. Leading the 9 entices a queen-king response, and, if successful, your following queen (for a pair if good fortune is smiling on you) runs the count to "29." This gives you an excellent opportunity for playing your aces back to back for four points. Playing defensively? Lead an ace (the diamond).

Playing the queen eliminates the possibility of playing the last three cards in sequence for a run of three. Jake may have a 3-3-2-queen (or any one "ten" card), leaving you with a 10-jack-king and egg on your face. When no obvious play is evident, keep combinations that count for you!

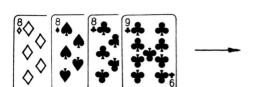 

As the non-dealer there's absolutely no advantage to leading a 9 here, saving the three 8's. It is mathematically impossible to play the three 8's in sequence. As a rule, always lead from three of a kind (exception: three aces, 2's, 3's with a lone 9 or a lone "ten" card). However, if you are the dealer, check your cards...perhaps you CAN play three in a sequence if the cards fall right for you!

71

# LITTLE TURKEY PLAYS

"Four"

"Twenty-three"

"Seven"

"Go"

"Fourteen"

"Twenty-eight"

Leading the 7 for your third play is a "turkey" play. Your 9 for "23" followed by Jake's 5 for "28" and a "go" almost positively eliminates the chances of Jake having an 8. Rarely will a player pass up a "31" play. Your third play should be the 8.

Leading the 4 when the starter card is a 3 is a "little turkey" boner, especially if the end-game pegging is involved and you are playing defensively. The 4 stands a 40% chance of being paired. The 3 cuts the odds of being paired to 27% (end game: no bias). The odds are a liitle less of this being a losing play early in the game. The 3 covers any "ten" response, as does the 4. However, if you are playing offensively, leading the 4 will draw a "ten" card response that you want more so than the 3. This is a subtle play, decided by whether you are playing offensively or defensively.

Oops. A golden opportunity has escaped. A chance to trade a run of three for a possible ten points has been passed up if you play the 4 instead of the 6 for your response to the 8 lead. The 6 is a good play, even if it's a single 6.

## *Summary*

Now we've gone over the game with some detail, picking up some points that surely will improve your game. You should be holding Uncle Jake to almost a standoff. He will still beat you 52 of 100 games, however, due to his experience, his faster play, and by playing the odds more consistently. Experience is hard to beat. You must practice your game and play regularly to sharpen your skills. By now you can nail Uncle Jake for his loose change if you double the wager when you have first deal, and cut the wager when he has first deal.

**At this point most books on cribbage come to an end. But I want to make you a winner.** *A standoff is simply not good enough.* **The next chapter, "Cribbage for the Expert," should be studied carefully. This will make you a winner!**

# Cribbage for the Expert

THE "TWENTY-SIX THEORY"
THE NON-DEALER'S PAR HOLES
THE DEALER'S PAR HOLES
THE NON-DEALER PLAYING THE THEORY
THE DEALER PLAYING THE THEORY
ANALYZING YOUR GAME
TALLYING YOUR GAMES

# Cribbage for the Expert

Now that you know how to run traps, play offense, play defense, fake flushes, dump jacks, entice the play, use psychological tricks, apply logic, and have a solid end game...what's left to learn? How can my game be improved to insure winning...even against an expert player?

Remember what Lord Kelvin said way back in the 19th Century:

> **"...that when you can measure what you are speaking about, and express it in numbers, you know something about it; but when you cannot express it in numbers, your knowledge is of a meager and unsatisfactory kind."**

To carry this thought a bit further, can you honestly say that you can play the first card of the very first hand with absolute certainty? And the second card? In fact, can you play the entire hand with absolute certainty? Do you know when to "play on?" When to "play off?" If not, your knowledge of cribbage IS of a meager and unsatisfactory kind!

Suppose you're the non-dealer. Your very first hand consists of the 4-5-queen-king. Do you know the correct card to lead? The 4? No. The correct card to open the game is the king.

You're the dealer and your first hand consists of the 4-5-6-king. Your opponent leads a king. Do you know the correct response? the 5 for "15-2?" Pair the king? No. The correct play is the 6. Both the king led by the non-dealer, and the 6 response by the dealer are made with absolute certainty.

But wait, earlier in this book, leading from a card lower than a 5 was recommended as the percentage play...the play with 57% less chance of your opponent scoring. And for the dealer, if the king is led, why not play a 5 for "15-2" or at least pair the king? Why lay off?

**Lead the King?**

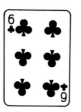

**And respond with 6?**

## The "Twenty-Six Theory"

An explanation of these controversial plays will come later. But first, I have developed a mathematical method of play that has been tried and proven, with thousands of games charted, tens of thousands of hands analyzed, and the results thoroughly studied. During this study, a method of play slowly evolved...a theory of play. A theory I have named the "Twenty-Six Theory."

This "Twenty-Six Theory," if played consistently, should improve your winning average a full 6%. Insignificant, you're thinking. But in this tough, subtle game of cribbage, 6% is the winning edge. Beating Uncle Jake by 6% is quite an achievement! Of course, players of lesser skill will fall at a much higher rate. On the tournament trail, my winning average is 58.1%...or a full 16.2% over breaking even, and this has been accomplished against highly skilled players. This winning percentage comes from consistently using the "Twenty-Six Theory."

By applying the "Twenty-Six Theory" your winning average will bound upwards against players of all skill levels. The "Twenty-Six Theory." the ultimate cribbage weapon! The weapon that tells you exactly what card to play...when to play it, almost without exception.

Remember the old "Law of Averages?" That law that has built the gambling empires, creating fortunes for the gambling houses? The law that beats you at roulette, beats you at the dice table, beats you at the black jack tables? This same law can work for you at cribbage, too. A Law of Averages operates in cribbage, just as surely as it operates in any card game.

But cribbage is a subtle card game...in fact, one of the most subtle card games devised by man. Players learn the basics quickly, and become competitive quickly. So quickly, in fact, that in a 121-point game, average players are actually dueling over the ten points or so (and usually much less) that can actually be controlled by the players, and not controlled by the luck of the draw. This small edge makes playing the "average" that much more important. Every point earned, or lost, through skillful, or unskillful play, is critical to winning consistently...or losing consistently. And this is where the "Twenty-Six Theory" comes in.

After compiling and averaging thousands of hands I found the average points scored and pegged by the non-dealer is 10.2. This same compiling and averaging gives the dealer (including pegging and scoring the crib) 16.2 points per deal. Every two deals, the average points add to 26.4. This is the basis of the Cribbage Law of Averages. And hence the name of my theory.

**Now, let's project these average points per deal around the 121-point board. First, the non-dealer: 10.2, 26.4, 36.6, 52.8, 63.0, 79.2, 89.4, 105.6, and on the ninth deal stands at 115.8.**

**Now the average points per deal for the dealer (remember, he has the first crib): 16.2, 26.4, 42.6, 52.8, 69.0, 79.2, 95.4, 105.6, and on the ninth deal stands at 121.8.**

The Cribbage Law of Averages dictates that the dealer will win the game by scoring his crib hand on the ninth deal. The non-dealer will be about five (5.2) points short after counting first on the ninth hand. And this crucial five points will, *on the average,* cause the non-dealer to lose 56 games of 100 (skill levels being equal, of course). These averages are the foundation of the "Twenty Six Theory."

The "Twenty-Six Theory" uses twenty-six as the average rather than twenty-seven (dropping the .4) because it's easier to slow a game (play off) than it is to speed up (play on) the game. It takes both players' cooperation to form runs, 15-2's, and pairs. However, if one player decides to play defense, and lays off forming runs, pairs and 15-2's, his opponent is stymied.

So, with twenty-six as the basis for the theory, let's once again project the players around the 121-point board.

---

**First, the non-dealer:**

**10 - 26 - 36 - 52 - 62 - 78 - 88 - 104 - 114**

After nine average deals, the non-dealer is 7 points short of winning the game.

---

**Secondly, projecting the dealer:**

**16 - 26 - 42 - 52 - 68 - 78 - 94 - 104 - 120**

After nine average deals, the dealer is *one point* short of winning the game, and more importantly, *has first count on the 10th deal.*

---

Playing the "Twenty-Six Theory," the dealer has the commanding edge in an average game, standing at 120 points after nine deals. The dealer will have first count on the 10th hand, and in control of the game. The average game gives the dealer the commanding

edge...the winning edge. Of course, the odds of playing an absolute average game are astronomical, but nevertheless, the **Cribbage Law of Averages** gives the dealer of the first hand the edge.

Well, you're thinking, so the odds are with me when I deal the first hand, and the odds are against me when I'm the non-dealer of the first hand. How do I pick up that extra 6% in winnings?

Once again, using the "Twenty-Six Theory," after nine *average* hands are completed, the non-dealer is seven points short of game. Seven tough points to peg on the 10th hand. The dealer, however, is one point short of game after counting his ninth hand and crib, needing but a single peg on the 10th hand, and has first count...a simple matter to win the game.

**Playing to this average, the basic strategy of the game becomes apparent. The non-dealer must play offense with his very first card played in the game. The dealer must play defense with his very first card played in the game!**

Why? The non-dealer must pick up an additional seven points over average during the nine-hand game to gain the advantage. And, of course, the more points picked up over average, the better. Having first count on the ninth hand and within easy distance (less than 10 points) of winning is the goal of the non-dealer.

The dealer, on the other hand, must play defense--slow the game down--to insure counting first on the 10th hand. The dealer has nine points (+9), he can sacrifice to defense and still maintain his advantage. Remember, after counting his hand and crib on the ninth hand, he is one point short of 121, and will average 10 points on the 10th hand (non-dealers average 10 points per deal).

Of course, as stated earlier, a game rarely, if ever, runs exactly average around the board. Adjustments must be made as the score fluctuates during the game. A player may begin (as the dealer) playing defense, but mat be forced into playing offense on the very next hand (if his first hand was a complete bust, scoring seven points or less). His strategy may swing back to defense later in the game if he scores a "barnburner," or if the game progresses at an extremely slow pace.

About one game in ten will run approximately average for the entire game. These are the games you must win! Whether you are the dealer or non-dealer on the first hand, these average games are yours. And this is your winning edge! These are the games the "Twenty-Six Theory" will win for you.

The non-average games will be won by the lucky recipient of the good cards...the good cuts for the starter card (skill levels being equal). But, nevertheless, having knowledge of the "Twenty-Six Theory" will greatly aid you in winning these non-average games as well. And the old Law of Averages will give you your share of the good cards, the good cuts for starters, and the pegging "breaks" will go your way as well.

But getting back to the average games, the "Twenty-Six Theory" will give you the 6% edge playing an expert...and a much greater edge against the average player. Against a beginner, it's downright devastating, with edges up to 50% or more (winning 75 of 100 games) not uncommon.

Let's begin a game with you being the non-dealer. Your objective is to speed up the game, to play offense...to gain those seven points over average to give you the advantage on the ninth deal.

Being the non-dealer, you, of course, discard to the dealer's crib on the first deal. *Contrary* to what was taught early in this book ("Beginning Cribbage"), don't

be overly concerned with balking the crib. Hold your hand to *score maximum count*...even at the expense of giving Uncle Jake a good crib. If Jake does get a high-scoring crib on the first deal, he still must make up 17 tough points over average to *count first and win on the eighth hand* (the dealer stands at 94 after seven average hands, and with first count on the eighth hand, scores an average 10 points, and will be at 104 points...17 points short of winning the game).

After discarding, and holding cards to form maximum count, begin pegging by leading a card that will entice a score, and allow you to retaliate with a score. Even if it means risking a pairs royal...or coming out on the short end of a run, **SCORE!** Take every pair, every run, every "15-2" possible!

Getting back to Lord Kelvin and the example of the 4-5-queen-king. The king is led! Why? Because the most likely card held by Jake will be a 5. The least likely "ten" card held by Jake will be a king. By leading the king, your chances of scoring are best. You hope to entice a 5 from Jake for "15-2" and then you counter with your 5 for a pair and two points. Even if Jake defies the odds and has the third 5 for pairs royal, running the count to "25," your 4 will probably gain the "go." You have scored three badly needed points...and even if

Jake had the third 5, and pegged eight points on the exchange, he is still far short of the 17 he needs to gain to win the game with first count on the eighth hand (if the game progresses approximately average.)

Leading the 4 from the 4-5-queen-king hand may draw a king or queen that you could pair for two points, running the count to "24," without much chance of a followup for "31" or a "go." But the odds are for a lower peg score, resulting in you NOT picking up many of those seven points (-7) over average you need to gain the advantage. **ON THE FIRST HAND AS THE NON-DEALER PLAY THE CARD THAT WILL RESULT IN THE MOST PEG POINTS POSSIBLE ... REGARDLESS OF THE NUMBER OF PEGS YOUR OPPONENT SCORES!**

If you are the dealer, the first hand should be played defensively. Your major objective is to hold your opponent scoreless on the peg. Lay off his lead; do not form runs, be extremely cautious about counting to "15-2"...especially on the first card lead.Try to keep cards to form the "Magic Eleven" to thwart the 10-card lead...even if it slightly weakens the count in your hand--PLAY DEFENSIVELY! Pat yourself on the back if Jake fails to peg a point on the first hand. You have done your duty if he is scoreless after pegging is completed. Remember, you can give up nine points (you are +9) and still have the advantage in an average game.

And once again, returning to Lord Kelvin and knowing your numbers, if Jake leads a king and you're holding 4-5-6-king, resist that temptation to play your 5 for a "15-2." Doubly resist the temptation to pair the king-- a pairs royal retaliation may well be fatal! The play is the 6 for "16," keeping the 5 (the other half of the "Magic Eleven") to score "31" in the case of the logical 10-card followup by Jake--resulting in only two points for you, but, more importantly, NO points for Jake. Continue to play defensively the remainder of the pegging on the first hand.

The only exception to this rule is if you have an extremely bad hand (two points or less...and the discards you have laid away in your crib are not helped by

the starter card, with the possibility that you have, indeed, lost your plus-nine advantage on the very first hand). In this event, peg cautiously, and score when you get no worse than a trade. Be especially cautious if Jake's first lead will combine with the starter card into a possible "barnburner." Before trading points on the peg, check his second card played. If it also combines with the starter card, avoid pegging, as a 12 or higher hand, plus a few pegs, will certainly put Jake in the driver's seat! If his third card played does not combine with the starter card, collect pegging points--but cautiously! There will, of course, be times when you have no alternative but to go ahead and peg, being trapped into a situation with no safe cards. Take your lumps, but keep them to a minimum.

Scoring throughout the game by the first-hand's non-dealer is more critical to the outcome of the game than is the scoring of the first-hands's dealer. Statistics show that the average game is nine hands (see the chapter "What's the Odds?"). The non-dealer scores first on this critical ninth hand and, after scoring, is about seven points short of winning the game (in a typical average game). One big hand (16 or more) scored during one of the nine deals will pick up those minus-seven points, providing the other eight hands are about average.

However, the dealer must score at least TWO big hands (16 or more) to gain the minus-seventeen points he must pick up to win the game with FIRST COUNT on the EIGHTH HAND! Picking up minus-seventeen in eight hands is much more difficult for the dealer than is picking up minus-seven points by the non-dealer in nine hands.

For this reason, the non-dealer's score is usually the key to the game. The dealer must make early efforts to slow the game down--to make the game ten hands. Or at least force the non-dealer to be no better than average, and as far below average as possible, by playing defensively throughout the game (or until board position dictates a shift in strategy). And, of course, the non-dealer must make every effort to speed the game--to make the game nine hands, and being in position (less than 10 points from the 121st hole) to take advantage of that ninth-hand first count.

Since the non-dealer's position throughout the game is usually more critical than the dealer's position, let's analyze the non-dealer's strategy. First, let's plot the board with marks, or targets to shoot for on each hand. This is the primary reason for playing an easy to read 121-point board. Since you (the non-dealer) must pick up seven points over average to be in first-count range of winning the game on the critical ninth deal, let's add seven points to the locations you should be during an average game. Set your goal for 17 as "par" on the first deal, then 33 as par on deal two, then 43, 59, 69, 85, 95, and finally 111 as "par" after completing the eighth deal.

Then, through playing offensively throughout the game, if you have attained or exceeded "par" 111 after playing the eighth deal, the odds of winning the game are in your favor. You are within 10 points of winning the game with first count, and the odds are even you will score at least 10 points as the non-dealer on the ninth deal. Of course, many games will NOT be average, but a compilation of statistics shows that *about 42% of all games are decided on the ninth deal.* Study the charts in the chapter "What's the Odds?" and you will understand why the ninth deal is so important in cribbage!

If you attain the "par" 111th hole after the eighth deal, you still have only a 50-50 chance of winning the game (if Jake maintains the pace with you). Still, 50-50 is better than losing those 12%, if the "Twenty-Six Theory" isn't played. But try to surpass the "par" holes by as many plus points as possible. With each point on the plus side of "par," your odds of winning increase.

For example, if you have scored 36 points after deal two, you are plus three to "par." If Jake, the dealer of the first hand, is tied with you at 36 points after the second deal, he is minus 7 to "par." Confusing? This minus 7 means he is *7 points under "par" to score 121 on first count on the eighth deal. The dealer of the first hand must speed up the game one full hand to gain that first count advantage* (or, if successful in slowing the game, will have that critical first-count advantage on the tenth deal). The first-hand dealer's target, or "par" for the second deal would be 43 (your third-hand target).

These numbers will be confusing at first, but mastery of board position is critical to expert cribbage. Don't give

up at this point. Take your time and study the "par" numbers. Remember, the non-dealer will have first count on ODD NUMBERED deals, the dealer will have first count on EVEN NUMBERED deals. And although the average game is nine deals, many games will go eight or ten deals. A few games will be won in seven or eleven deals. About one game in 300 will be won in six deals...with a twelve-deal game not quite as rare. A thirteen-deal game is about a 1,000 to 1 shot. The shortest game in some 60,000 games witnessed is a five-deal game (three have been witnessed by the author). The reason longer games are not as rare as short games is that poor, low-counting hands are more common than those high-counting "barnburners" (suspicions confirmed?), and by the fact it is easier to slow a game down than to speed it up.

Study the "par" holes on the next two pages. Memorize the "par" holes...both for the non-dealer and the dealer. Note the position of the "par" holes when you will be the non-dealer and having first count. The game may be a very slow game...or a very fast game...and you will have to re-adjust your game, perhaps several times, to maintain your advantage, or trying to attain an advantage. Many games will be played that the luck of the draw simply forbid your winning, despite all your efforts of maintaining, or attaining, board position.

But, by playing to these "par" holes to attain board position you will improve your winning average. Over average players, you should win an extra 12 games in every hundred played! *And that's the wining edge!*

After thoroughly studying the "par" holes on the next two pages, let's play a couple of games on paper. Once, as the non-dealer, and another as the dealer. Each hand will be summarized as to the type of thinking that should be employed as you make your way though the games. Each game will be reviewed upon completion. And after these exercises in board play, your insight to winning cribbage should be sharpened. And your winning average should begin to rise dramatically. Two national champions have employed these numbers to achieve even greater success...and I have used these "par" holes to win two national titles, and seven All-American ratings! And I'm sure they will help you to *play winning cribbage!*

# The Non-Dealer's Par Holes

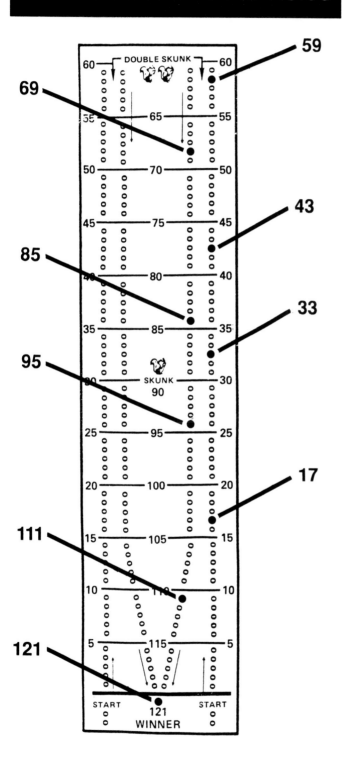

## Non-Dealer's Par*

**Deal 1:** 17 (first count)

**Deal 2:** 33

**Deal 3:** 43 (first count)

**Deal 4:** 59

**Deal 5:** 69 (first count)

**Deal 6:** 85

**Deal 7:** 95 (first count)

**Deal 8:** 111

**Deal 9:** 121 (first count)

*Par for an average game. Par may change in an extremely fast or slow game. Attaining these "par" holes give you a 50-50 chance of winning the game. Make every effort to exceed these numbers, without giving up board position.

## The Dealer's Par Holes

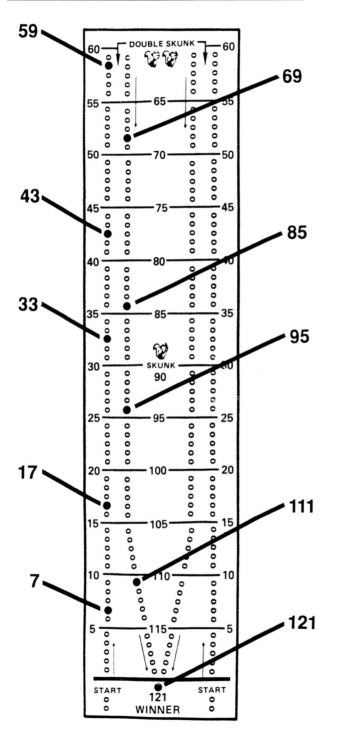

## Dealer's Par*

**Deal 1:** 7

**Deal 2:** 17 (first count)

**Deal 3:** 33

**Deal 4:** 43 (first count)

**Deal 5:** 59

**Deal 6:** 69 (first count)

**Deal 7:** 85

**Deal 8:** 95 (first count)

**Deal 9:** 111

**Deal 10:** 121 (first count)

*Par for an average game. Par may change in an extremely fast or slow game. Attaining these "par" holes give you a 50-50 chance of winning the game. Make every effort to exceed these numbers, without giving up board position.

84

## *Playing the "Twenty-Six Theory"*

Let's play two typical games using the "Twenty-Six Theory." Once as the non-dealer, and then another as the dealer. By playing these two games on "paper," you should get a "feel" for playing to the "par holes" that is essential to play winning cribbage.

Play will be summarized after each deal, and reviewed upon completion of the game.

# Deal one. As the non-dealer you are -7. Your par is 17.

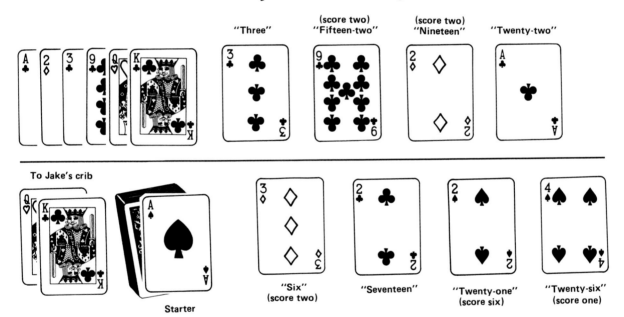

**Summary: as the non-dealer, your objective is maximum score.** By holding the 9 instead of the queen you cover the 3 lead for maximum pegging score (many players mistakenly discard the 9-king as balking cards to Jake's crib). Despite the 9 peg points scored by Jake, your total score of 16 points (-1) vs. Jake's total of 22 points (three point crib) makes the game a virtual tossup at this point. Jake is -11 for an eight-hand game try, but +15 for scoring first count on the tenth deal. Your score at this point is the key to the game. -1 to average for winning on the ninth deal (with first count).

**Deal one.**
**Your score: 16 (-1).**
**Jake's score: 22 (-11).**

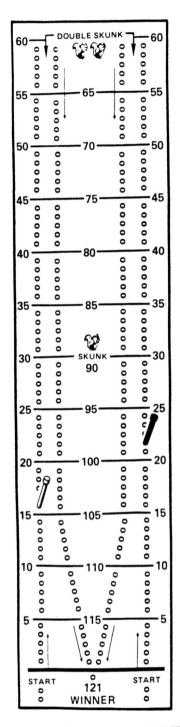

In all graphics, your pegs are WHITE, Jake's pegs are BLACK

## Deal two
## You are -1 (your crib)
## Jake is -11
## Your par is 33

Starter

To your crib

| "Ten" | (score four) "Twenty-two, for four" | (score two) "Thirty-one" | (score one) "Twelve" |

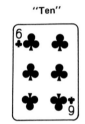   

| "Four" | "Fifteen, for five" (score five) | "Twenty-three" | "Ten" |

Summary: Jake's 4 lead is not matched by the starter 9 (Jake's maximum hand is 16) allowing you to try enticing Jake's 5 for a "sucker play." If Jake has a 5, your 7 scores a run of four (a good trade since you are -1 and Jake is -11). In this case, the play worked to your advantage as you scored seven peg points vs. Jake's five peg points.

Assuming you scored six points with the crib hand, your total score for deal two is 23 points. You are now standing at 39 (+6). Jake, after scoring 11, now stands at 33 (-10). The odds are now in your favor of winning the game.

## Deal two.
## Your score: 39 (+6)
## Jake's score: 33 (-10)

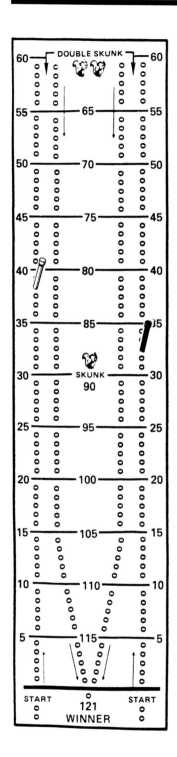

## Deal three
## You are +6
## Jake is -10 and has the crib
## Your par is 43

Starter

To Jake's crib

"Three"     "Twenty-three"     "Ten"     (score three) "Thirty, and a pair"

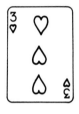

"Go"

"Thirteen"     "Twenty-eight" (score one)     "Twenty"     "Ten" (score one)

Summary: keeping the 3 instead of the king is a percentage play. Leading a king has a 66% risk of being scored upon (no bias) vs. only a 28% risk (no bias) when a lone 3 is led. The 3 may be answered by a "ten" card that could be safely paired by you (in the example, alas, Jake played a king). Since you are +6, you "dump" the jack as your second play. If you were minus to par, the jack would be held for desperation offense, hoping to pair Jake's jack later, if possible. Your total score for deal three is six points. You stand at 45 (+2). Jake scored a six-point crib and totaled 17 points. Standing at 50, Jake is now -9. Your advantage dwindled somewhat but you are still in the driver's seat. Your strategy is still offense (maximum).

## Deal three.
## Your score: 45 (+2)
## Jake's score: 50 (-9)

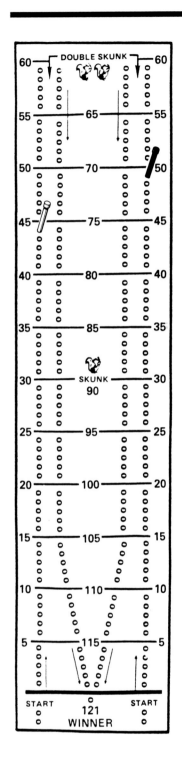

## Deal four
## You are +2 (your crib)
## Jake is -9
## Your par is 59

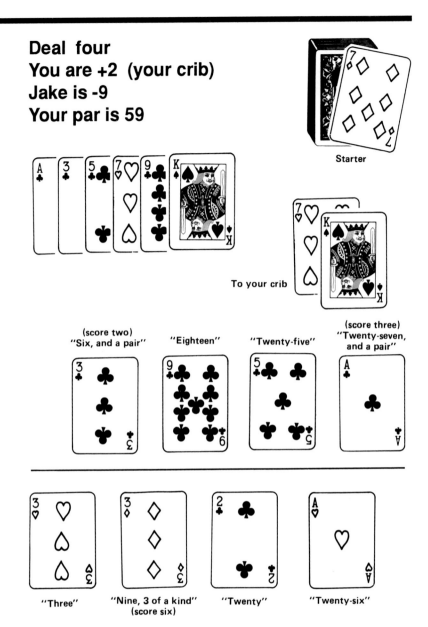

Starter

To your crib

(score two)
"Six, and a pair"  "Eighteen"  "Twenty-five"  (score three)
"Twenty-seven, and a pair"

"Three"  "Nine, 3 of a kind"  "Twenty"  "Twenty-six"
(score six)

Summary: playing for maximum, you hold the club flush and pair Jake's 3 lead (ignoring the threat of a pairs royal retaliation). Pegging five, scoring a hand valued at eight, and a five-point crib adds to 18 total points. You now stand at 63 (+4). Jake scored six peg points and a ten hand, placing him at 66 (-3). Jake trimmed your advantage from 11 to 7. Greater care must be exercised with deal five. Your strategy is still offense, but with discretion.

## Deal four.
## Your score: 63 (+4)
## Jake's score: 66 (-3)

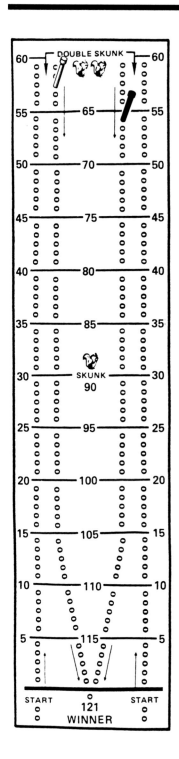

## Deal five
## You are +4
## Jake is -3 and has the crib
## Your par is 69

Starter

To Jake's crib

| "One" | (score two) "Thirteen" | "Twenty" | "Go" "Four" |
|---|---|---|---|

 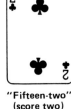  

"Seven" | "Fifteen-two" (score two) | "Twenty-eight" (score one) | "Eleven" (score one)

Summary: playing maximum, your discard to Jake's crib would be the pair of aces. Caution must be exercised as Jake is only -3 of winning in *eight* deals. Keeping the ace-4-5-6 for an almost sure seven point hand (only a 2 starter misses this hand), maintaining par or better (69). You lead the "safe" ace. Jake's 6 response does *not* combine with the starter king making your 6 pair a less risky play. If the starter were a 5-6-7 or 9 you would be wise to lay off the pair as Jake may well have a barnburner, picking up his -3 to par and winning in eight deals. You score 11 points and stand at 74 (+5). Jake scored a three-point crib, four peg points and a seven point hand and stands at 80 (-5). Deal five strengthened your advantage. Your strategy remains the same: offense with discretion.

## Deal five.
## Your score: 74 (+5)
## Jake's score: 80 (-5)

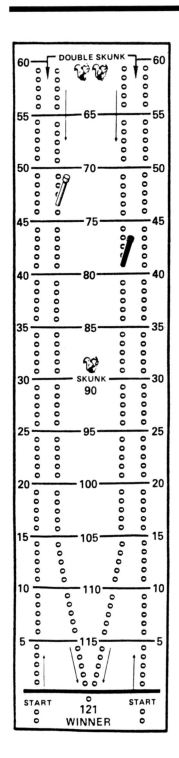

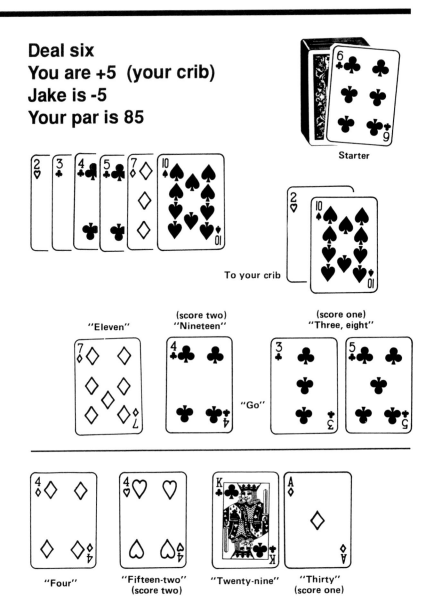

# Deal six
## You are +5 (your crib)
## Jake is -5
## Your par is 85

Starter

To your crib

"Eleven"

(score two)
"Nineteen"

(score one)
"Three, eight"

"Go"

"Four"

"Fifteen-two"
(score two)

"Twenty-nine"

"Thirty"
(score one)

Summary: discarding the 2-10 allows you to keep the 4-7 ("Magic Eleven") and a 3 starter will score a maximum 14 points. You lay off Jake's 4 lead as a pairs royal response by Jake (-5) may well be fatal. However, pairing his second 4 is a percentage play. Your crib counted only two points for your total count of 14. Standing at 88, you are now +3.

Jake's 11 points puts him at 91 (-4). And once again, despite the fact that Jake has the lead (three points), you have the advantage. Your strategy for deal seven? Offense with discretion.

## Deal six.
## Your score: 88 (+3)
## Jake's score: 91 (-4)

## Deal seven
## You are +3
## Jake is -4 and has the crib
## Your par is 95

Starter

To Jake's crib

"Four"

(score two)
"Fifteen-two"

"Twenty-six"

(score two)
"Thirty-one"

"Fourteen"

"Sixteen"
(score two)

"Go"

"Ten, twenty"
(score one)

Summary: you discard offensively, holding for maximum score. The starter doubles your count and insures you of reaching at least "par" (95). Since par is assured, you lead *defensively* (Jake is only -4) with the 4. Your score for deal seven totals 13 and you are standing at 101 (+6). Jake scored a six-point crib for a total of 17, and is now standing at 108 (-3). Deal eight must be played with extreme caution as Jake has about one chance in four of scoring 13 points to win the game (and he has first count). Unless your eighth deal hand is a complete bust, defense is the byword.

## Deal seven.
## Your score: 101 (+6)
## Jake's score: 108 (-3)

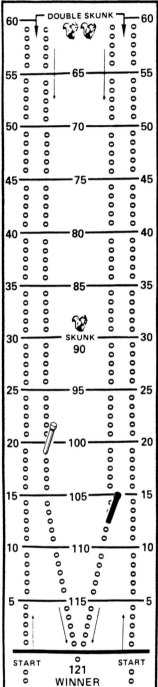

## Deal eight
## You are +6 (your crib)
## Jake is -3
## Your par is 111

**Starter**

**To your crib**

"Eighteen"

(score two)
"Thirty-one"

"Seventeen"

(score one)
"Twenty-six"

"Ten"

"Twenty-eight"

"Ten"

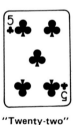

"Twenty-two"

Summary: since you are +6 and Jake is threatening to win the game, deal eight must be played defensively. Discard the 5-king, keeping *two* "Magic Eleven" combinations (3-8 and 4-7). Your objective is to hold Jake scoreless pegging. Jake scores no pegging points and an eight-point hand. Standing at 116, Jake is 5 points short of winning the game. You score 14 points (four-point crib) and are now standing at 115 (+4). Deal nine must be played with extreme caution. End-game pegging will be a critical factor.

## Deal eight.
## Your score: 115 (+4)
## Jake's score: 116 (-5)

92

## Deal nine
## You are +4 and have first count
## Jake is -5
## Your par is 121 and game

Starter

To Jake's crib

"Four"          "Twelve, pairs royal for six and game!"

(score six)

"Eight"
(score two)

Summary: pegging defensively, you must lead from a small pair (ace-2-3-4) if possible. Good fortune smiled upon you with a pair of 4's. Keep the jack of clubs to match your 4 of clubs lead to keep a flush fake opportunity intact. Should Jake lay off the 4 lead? No. Jake must gamble to win the game by pegging. He knows *the non-dealer will score* *at least six points about 88 times of 100* (see charts in "What's the Odds" chapter). Playing the "Twenty-Six Theory" early in the game kept the odds in your favor in this tight, *average* nine-deal game, and rewarded you with a three-point victory!

## Deal nine.
## You win 121-118!

Let's review the game we've just played. Manipulating a game of cribbage on paper as we have just done to come up with a desired result is, of course, easy. However, about four games in ten will be played somewhat like the game illustrated. The game was decided on the ninth deal by end-game pegging. And by playing the "Twenty-Six Theory," the non-dealer of the first hand won the game. In this near-average game many players--even very good players--would have *lost* by playing conservatively early in the game.

For example, risking a high-counting crib for Jake in deal one (king-queen discard) in order to "cover" your 3 lead with your 9 was rewarded with two peg points. The "sucker" play in deal two (4-6-5-7), resulting in seven peg points, was the key play of the game, helping you attain a +6 at that point. Despite being behind after playing hand three (50-45) the odds remained in your favor throughout the remainder of the game. *Playing the "Twenty-Six Theory" the non-dealer was in range of winning the game with first count on the ninth deal.*

## *Playing the "Twenty-Six Theory" as the Dealer*

Now, let's go through a few typical game situations played by the dealer of the first hand. Since the dealer is +9 before the first card is played, and will count first on the tenth deal, defense is the byword. Your objective is to keep that +9 on the plus side of the ledger and Jake on the minus side (Jake starts at -7, of course).

Your game must be geared to board position at all times...playing the averages. There will be times when you and Jake are both near zero to the "par" holes. Your strategy then is governed by your hand, the starter card, and whether Jake's first, or second, card match the starter card (a potential barnburner!). Early in the game, the general rule is play offense if there is a doubt about whether to play offense or defense (both players are close to "par"). This general rule is valid for both the dealer and the non-dealer. However, in the later stages of the game, the general rule is to play defense. But again, check Jake's lead, the starter card, and your hand. Consider the discard to the crib, especially in relation to the starter card. And does Jake's first lead minimize the crib being a barnburner (if it's Jake's crib)? You must thoroughly consider the crib possibilities before committing yourself to offense or defense in the later stages of a tight game (and it's a good practice early in the game, too.)

The reason for the shift in strategy in the later stages of the game is that it is easier to slow the game down than it is to speed it up. If you gamble offensively early in the game and fail, there will be ample time to work on your defense and still win the game. However, if you gamble offensively in the later stages of the game, and fail, you will have lost control of the game.

Once again, study the odds in the following chapter "What's the Odds?" pertaining to average points scored per hand (the non-dealer's) and average points scored by the dealer (including the crib). These odds will give you the necessary insight on when to gamble and play offensively, and when to play defensively. And remember, hunch players are losers! Play the odds!

Let's review a few hands, analyzing the strategy of the dealer of the first hand... playing the "Twenty-Six Theory."

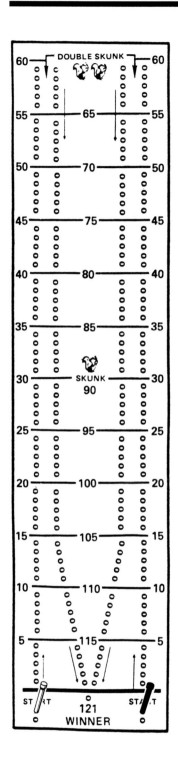

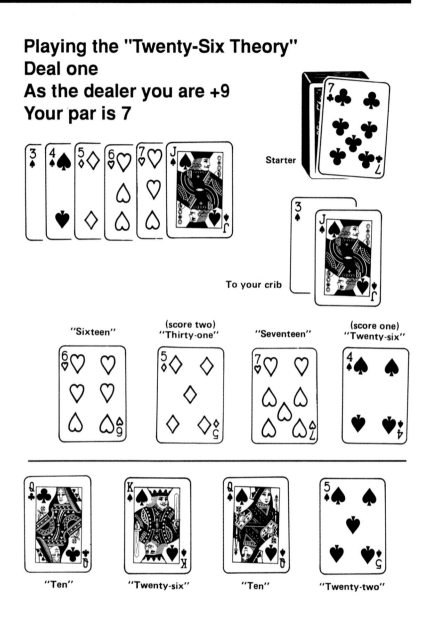

## Playing the "Twenty-Six Theory"
## Deal one
## As the dealer you are +9
## Your par is 7

**Starter**

**To your crib**

"Sixteen"    (score two) "Thirty-one"    "Seventeen"    (score one) "Twenty-six"

"Ten"    "Twenty-six"    "Ten"    "Twenty-two"

Summary: as the dealer your goal is to hold the non-dealer score-less pegging. Do not destroy your hand in discarding to your crib, however, in an attempt to keep defensive pegging cards. But peg defensively! Hold Jake scoreless if at all possible. In the hand illustrated, playing a 6 of Jake's queen lead holds Jake score-less. You have sacrificed two points in the process, but the defensive trade is to the dealer's advantage (+9). Remember, Jake, as the non-dealer is -7 to par. You succeed in holding Jake scoreless pegging. Jake's score: 8 points (-9). Your crib contained 6 points and after deal one you stand at 21 (+14).

## Deal one.
## Your score: 21 (+14)
## Jake's score: 8 (-9)

95

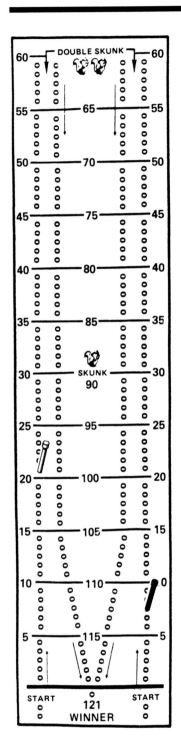

## Deal two
## You are + 14
## Jake is -9 and has the crib
## Your par is 17 (or 43 for an 8-deal game)

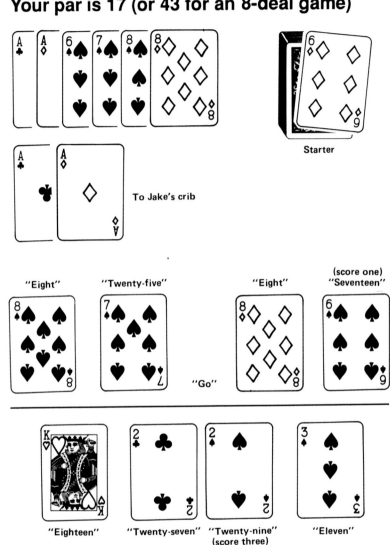

To Jake's crib

Starter

"Eight"  "Twenty-five"  "Eight"  (score one) "Seventeen"

"Go"

"Eighteen"  "Twenty-seven"  "Twenty-nine" (score three)  "Eleven"

Summary: cutting the starter 6 changes your strategy from defense to offense. You now have an excellent chance to "run for eight" (try to win in 8 deals). You peg only one point (despite your efforts to score) and stand at 42 (-1 for an 8-deal try, or a whopping +25 for a 10-deal game).

Jake totaled 9 points and stands at only 17 (-16). The advantage is obviously yours with the option to play either defense or offense, depending on how the cards fall on deal three.

## Deal two.
## Your score: 42 (-1 or +25).
## Jake's score: 17 (-16).

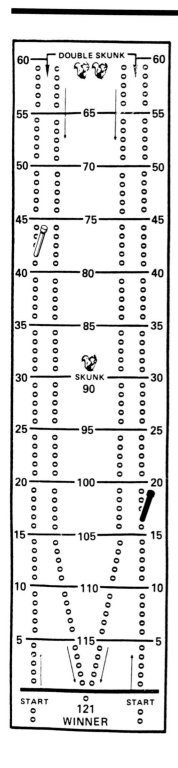

# Deal three
# You are -1 or +25 (your crib)
# Jake is -16
# Your par is 59 (8-deal try)

Starter

To your crib

(score two) "Fifteen-two"   "Twenty-nine"   (score two) "Thirty-one"   "Eighteen"

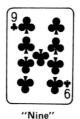

"Nine"   "Twenty-five"   "Ten"   "Twenty-eight" (score one)

Summary: Ouch! You are dealt a poor hand and score a total of 10 points (6-point crib) and stand at 52 (-7 for an 8-deal try). Jake scored an average 10 points and stands at only 27 and is still -16. Your strategy remains the same. You have the option of playing offensively or defensively on deal four.

Deal three.
Your score: 52 (-7 or +19).
Jake's score: 27 (-16).

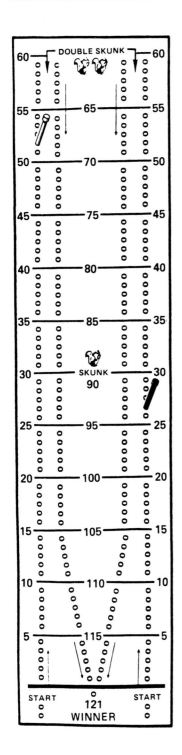

## Deal four
## You are -7 or +19
## Jake is -16 and has the crib
## Your par is 69 (8- deal try)

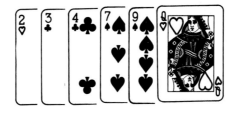

Starter

To Jake's crib

| "Three" | "Sixteen" | "Twenty-four" | "Go" "Four" |
|---------|-----------|---------------|-------------|

| "Seven" | "Twenty-two" | "Twenty-nine" (score one) | "Ten" (score one) |
|---------|--------------|---------------------------|-------------------|

  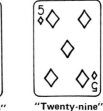 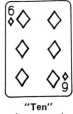

Summary: the starter card did not give you a high-scoring hand and, in addition, Jake's first card played (4) may combine with the starter (giving him a possible high-scoring hand). Those two circumstances force you to play the defensive option. You do NOT pair Jake's 4 or form a run of 3 as defense is now the byword. Jake, indeed, does have a high-scoring 24-point hand, pegs 2 points, and has a 8-point crib for a total of 34 points!

You score only 6 points and stand at 58 (-11 for a 8-deal try or +15 for a 10-deal try). Jake, alas, stands at 61 (+2). Your option has disappeared. Defense is the play for deal 5.

## Deal four.
## Your score: 58 (-11 or +15).
## Jake's score: 61 (+2).

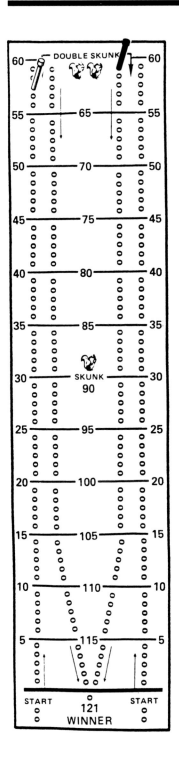

# Deal five
## You are -11 or +15 (your crib)
## Jake is +2
## Your par is 59 (10-deal try)

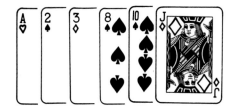

Starter

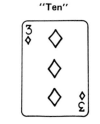

To your crib

| "Ten" | "Nineteen" | (score one) "Twenty-eight" | (score one) "Fourteen" |

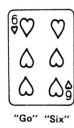

| "Seven" | "Seventeen" | "Twenty-seven" | "Go" "Six" |

Summary: playing defensively, you discard the 10-jack, keeping the 8-3 "eleven" combination intact (in the event Jake leads a "ten" card). Jake leads a 7, and playing defensively, you respond with your safest card (your 3). You continue to peg defensively and fortunately Jake fails to score. Unfortunately, Jake has a 12-point hand and now stands at 73 (+4).

You score 4 points in your crib and now stand at 69 (+10). Trying for an 8-deal game at this point would be foolish. Continue playing defensively on deal 6.

**Deal five.**
**Your score: 69 (+10).**
**Jake's score: 73 (+4).**

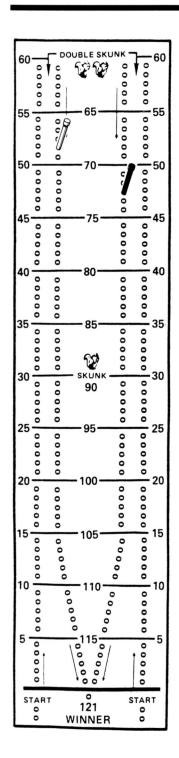

## Deal six
## You are +10
## Jake is +4 and has the crib
## Your par is 69

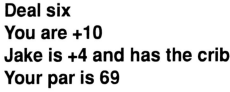

Starter

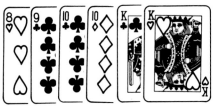

To Jake's crib

| "Ten" | (score three)<br>"Twenty-eight" | "Sixteen" | (score one)<br>"Thirty" |
|---|---|---|---|

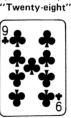  

---

 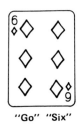  

"Nineteen"          "Go" "Six"          "Twenty-two"          "Go" "Four"<br>(score one)

Summary: break up a double run? Yes. Jake is +4 and defense is critical. By discarding from your pairs, you cut Jake's odds of scoring in the crib. Your par is 69 and you are standing at 69. Your score is not critical to the game's outcome. Your king is the safe lead and will give you the best chance to peg safely. After seeing two kings, Jake will score on a king lead 57% of the time (no bias). Leading from a lone 8? Jake will score 65% of the time (no bias). See page 60.

Holding Jake to a minimum of one peg point, and only a 2-point crib makes your play of the hand a success. Jake scored a total of 11 points and stands at 84 (-1). You scored only 7 points, but, more importantly, you have regained the advantage of +7.

## Deal six.
## Your score: 76 (+7).
## Jake's score: 84 (-1).

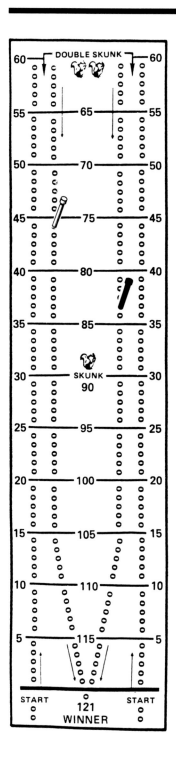

## Deal seven
## You are +7 (your crib)
## Jake is -1
## Your par is 85

Starter

To your crib

| "Nineteen" | "Thirty" | (score four) "Thirty-one" | "Sixteen" |
|---|---|---|---|

"Ten"     "Twenty-nine"     "Go"     "Ten"     "Twenty-six" (score one)

**Summary:** holding the ace-ace-9 ("Magic Eleven") to peg defensively was successful. Jake scored only one peg point and an 8-point hand for a total of 9 points. Standing at 93, Jake is now -2. Your crib totaled only 4 points and your total score for deal seven was 12 (standing at 88.)

You are now +3. Your strategy for deal eight is offense, but with caution.

## Deal seven.
## Your score: 88 (+3).
## Jake's score: 93 (-2).

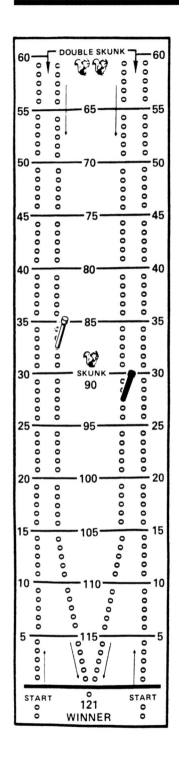

## Deal eight
## You are +3
## Jake is -2 and has the crib
## Your par is 95

Starter

To Jake's crib

"Three"

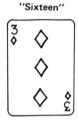

"Sixteen"

(score two)
"Thirty-one"

"Fourteen"

"Thirteen"

"Twenty-six"

"Ten"

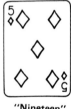

"Nineteen"
(score one)

Summary: the starter card gave you a 14-point hand to insure exceeding par 95. Your strategy (with par assured) is defensive pegging. Leading your safe 3 and dumping the 5 for thirty-one (sacrificing a point) are good defensive plays. Jake is held to a single point pegging (minimum for the dealer). Your total score of 16 puts you at 104 (+9). Jake scores a 4-point crib and scores a near-average 15 points.

Jake stands at 108 (-3). Needing 13 to win the game on deal nine, Jake has about a 26% chance to win the game (see charts in the next chapter).

## Deal eight.
## Your score: 104 (+9).
## Jake's score: 108 (-3).

102

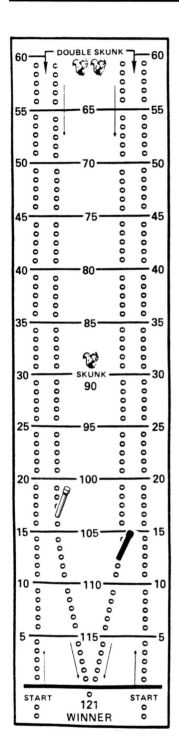

## Deal nine
## You are +9 (your crib)
## Jake is -3
## Your par is 111

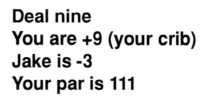

Starter

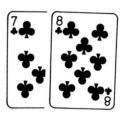

To your crib

| "Thirteen" | "Twenty-five" | "Three" | (score one) "Eleven" |
|---|---|---|---|
|  |  |  |  |

|  |  |  |  |
|---|---|---|---|
| "Four" | "Twenty-three" | "Thirty-one" (score two) | "Eight" |

Summary: once again the starter card assured you of exceeding par 111, allowing you to peg defensively. Jake scored an average 11 points and is 2 points short of winning the game. The crib contained 6 points and your total score for deal nine is 21 points...more than enough to win the game. Playing defensively, after Jake's high-scoring deal four, has won the game for you. The Cribbage Law of Averages and the "Twenty-six Theory" has rewarded you with another "squeeker" victory!

103

## Reviewing the Game

Reviewing the game, we find how a high-scoring hand by either player can change strategy from defense to offense and back again. Your high-scoring second hand (21 points as the non-dealer) gave you the option of offensive or defensive play. Jake's 24-point fourth deal hand regained the advantage in Jake's favor, and your play was defensive for the remainder of the game. And despite Jake scoring average, or near-average hands from that point on, your defensive pegging strategy (a decision based on the "Twenty-six Theory's" par points) rewarded you with a narrow victory.

Of course, the game was manipulated, with a favorable outcome. Many games will not be played as closely to average as the game illustrated. Time and time again your strategy will backfire. But hang in there. That old Cribbage Law of Averages and the "Twenty-six Theory" will pay off! It should reward you with an increase of about 6% in your winning edge. And playing opponents like Jake the Snake, that's the winning edge!

Now you have the complete game! The only missing ingredient is your analysis of *your own game.* Begin an analysis of *all* your games, with *all* your opponents. Keep running averages of games, points scored per hand, your winning percentage against each player, and your average point margin of victory (or, heaven forbid, your average point margin of losing). Work to improve your averages. Analyze your game thoroughly. You'll be amazed how these "dry" statistics will begin to pay off for you. You may discover that your averages are slightly different from the "Twenty-six Theory." In fact, cribbage experts differ on their opinion of the averages. They range from "Twenty-five" up to "Twenty-nine" for a two-hand average. Keep your own scores. If your average differs widely, you may want to play your own theory.

But, whatever you do, make Lord Kelvin proud of you. Keep a book on all your opponents. A quick, easy way to keep a running record is to mark your winning games with the score, and number of points you won by (Jake is beaten, and ends in the 101st hole...mark "20" in your book), and mark your losses with the number of points you lose by...and circle that number...a very quick, simple process. Get in the habit of playing with your book, and in your leisure time, analyze the results.

The next chapter will give you some insight as to the odds of scoring in cribbage, and what your winning...or losing...averages means in terms of what you can expect to win...or lose...in this frustratingly simple game of cribbage! This fascinating, exciting game of cribbage!

# What's the Odds

# What's the Odds?

Many games of cribbage are won or lost by simply **knowing the odds** and playing the hand accordingly. Study the next few pages and you will improve your knowledge of cribbage probabilities. These probability tidbits are especially helpful when playing those last crucial hands...and that crucial end-game pegging that decides so many games.

Remember, hunch players are losers. Play the odds, and sooner or later you will be rewarded with the majority of victories.

The charts are based on samples of 1,000 or more. Your own games should parallel these findings. Of course, millions of games would have to be analyzed to pinpoint these probabilities precisely. And this is what makes cribbage such an exciting game...the endless combinations of cards and pegging possibilities.

The chart to the right analyzes the numbers of deals in a typical cribbage game, and who has the advantage (the dealer or the non-dealer). The chart shows that a nine-deal game is by far the most common (about 42% of all games are played in nine deals). The lower chart shows that the dealer wins about 19% more than the non-dealer (250-170) in a nine-deal game. It also shows that about 90% of all games are played in eight, nine, or ten deals. But the ninth deal is the critical deal. In an **average** game, the non-dealer comes up about five points short, and the dealer wins...usually by counting his crib to win the game. **By using the "Twenty-six Theory" as your guide, you can cut the dealer's ninth deal advantage.**

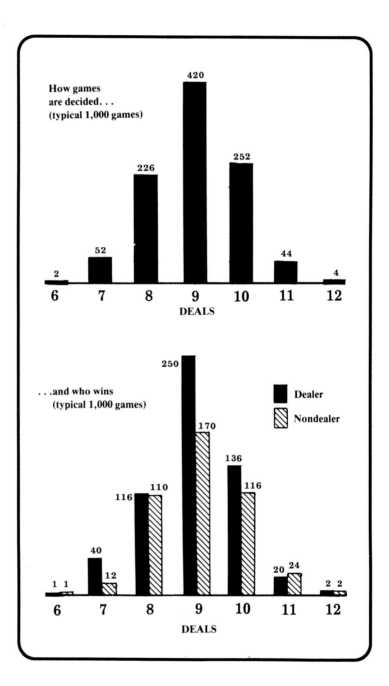

How games are decided. . .
(typical 1,000 games)

. . .and who wins
(typical 1,000 games)

■ Dealer
▨ Nondealer

107

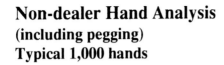

## Non-dealer Hand Analysis
### (including pegging)
### Typical 1,000 hands

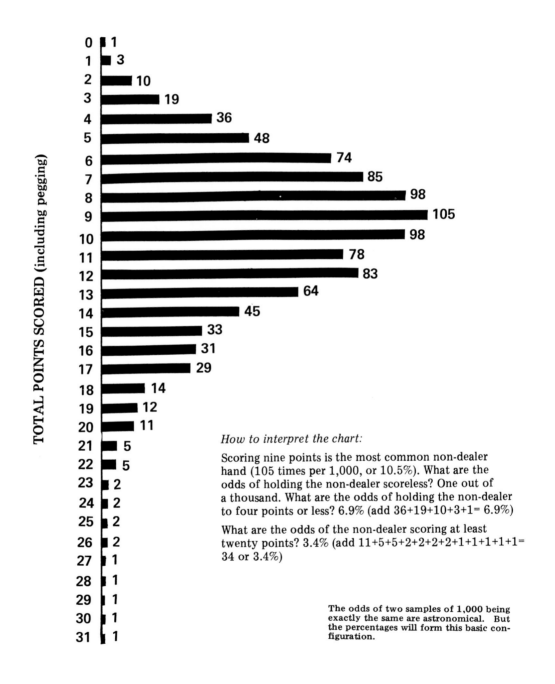

**TOTAL POINTS SCORED** (including pegging)

| Points | Frequency |
|--------|-----------|
| 0 | 1 |
| 1 | 3 |
| 2 | 10 |
| 3 | 19 |
| 4 | 36 |
| 5 | 48 |
| 6 | 74 |
| 7 | 85 |
| 8 | 98 |
| 9 | 105 |
| 10 | 98 |
| 11 | 78 |
| 12 | 83 |
| 13 | 64 |
| 14 | 45 |
| 15 | 33 |
| 16 | 31 |
| 17 | 29 |
| 18 | 14 |
| 19 | 12 |
| 20 | 11 |
| 21 | 5 |
| 22 | 5 |
| 23 | 2 |
| 24 | 2 |
| 25 | 2 |
| 26 | 2 |
| 27 | 1 |
| 28 | 1 |
| 29 | 1 |
| 30 | 1 |
| 31 | 1 |

*How to interpret the chart:*

Scoring nine points is the most common non-dealer hand (105 times per 1,000, or 10.5%). What are the odds of holding the non-dealer scoreless? One out of a thousand. What are the odds of holding the non-dealer to four points or less? 6.9% (add 36+19+10+3+1= 6.9%)

What are the odds of the non-dealer scoring at least twenty points? 3.4% (add 11+5+5+2+2+2+2+1+1+1+1+1= 34 or 3.4%)

The odds of two samples of 1,000 being exactly the same are astronomical. But the percentages will form this basic configuration.

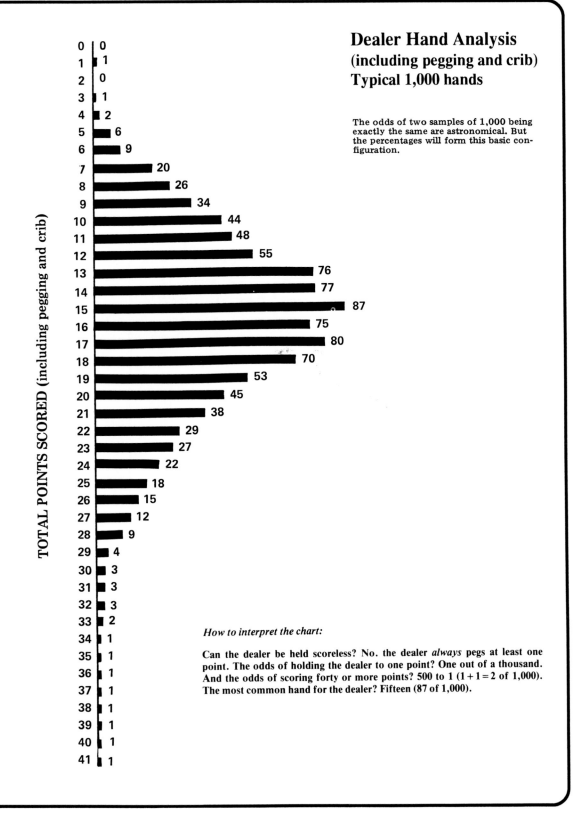

**Dealer Hand Analysis**
(including pegging and crib)
Typical 1,000 hands

The odds of two samples of 1,000 being exactly the same are astronomical. But the percentages will form this basic configuration.

TOTAL POINTS SCORED (including pegging and crib)

| Points | Hands |
|--------|-------|
| 0 | 0 |
| 1 | 1 |
| 2 | 0 |
| 3 | 1 |
| 4 | 2 |
| 5 | 6 |
| 6 | 9 |
| 7 | 20 |
| 8 | 26 |
| 9 | 34 |
| 10 | 44 |
| 11 | 48 |
| 12 | 55 |
| 13 | 76 |
| 14 | 77 |
| 15 | 87 |
| 16 | 75 |
| 17 | 80 |
| 18 | 70 |
| 19 | 53 |
| 20 | 45 |
| 21 | 38 |
| 22 | 29 |
| 23 | 27 |
| 24 | 22 |
| 25 | 18 |
| 26 | 15 |
| 27 | 12 |
| 28 | 9 |
| 29 | 4 |
| 30 | 3 |
| 31 | 3 |
| 32 | 3 |
| 33 | 2 |
| 34 | 1 |
| 35 | 1 |
| 36 | 1 |
| 37 | 1 |
| 38 | 1 |
| 39 | 1 |
| 40 | 1 |
| 41 | 1 |

*How to interpret the chart:*

**Can the dealer be held scoreless? No. the dealer *always* pegs at least one point. The odds of holding the dealer to one point? One out of a thousand. And the odds of scoring forty or more points? 500 to 1 (1 + 1 = 2 of 1,000). The most common hand for the dealer? Fifteen (87 of 1,000).**

## Dealer and Non-dealer Scoring Odds

| What's the odds of holding the non-dealer: | | What's the odds of the non-dealer scoring: | |
|---|---|---|---|
| *Points* | *Odds* | *Points (or more)* | *Odds* |
| 0 | 1,000 to 1 | 31 | 1,000 to 1 |
| 1 | 250 to 1 | 30 | 500 to 1 |
| 2 | 70 to 1 | 29 | 333 to 1 |
| 3 | 33 to 1 | 28 | 250 to 1 |
| 4 | 14 to 1 | 27 | 200 to 1 |
| 5 | 8½ to 1 | 26 | 143 to 1 |
| 6 | 5 to 1 | 25 | 111 to 1 |
| 7 | 4 to 1 | 24 | 91 to 1 |
| 8 | 2½ to 1 | 23 | 77 to 1 |
| 9 | Even | 22 | 56 to 1 |
| | | 21 | 44 to 1 |
| | | 20 | 29 to 1 |
| | | 19 | 22 to 1 |
| | | 18 | 17 to 1 |
| | | 17 | 11 to 1 |
| | | 16 | 8 to 1 |
| | | 15 | 7 to 1 |
| | | 14 | 5 to 1 |
| | | 13 | 4 to 1 |
| | | 12 | 3 to 1 |
| | | 11 | 2½ to 1 |
| | | 10 | Even |

**Including pegging**

| What's the odds of holding the dealer: | | What's the odds of the dealer scoring: | |
|---|---|---|---|
| *Points* | *Odds* | *Points (or more)* | *Odds* |
| 0 | Not Possible | 41 | 1,000 to 1 |
| 1 | 1,000 to 1 | 40 | 500 to 1 |
| 2 | 800 to 1 | 39 | 333 to 1 |
| 3 | 500 to 1 | 38 | 250 to 1 |
| 4 | 250 to 1 | 37 | 200 to 1 |
| 5 | 100 to 1 | 36 | 167 to 1 |
| 6 | 53 to 1 | 35 | 143 to 1 |
| 7 | 21 to 1 | 34 | 125 to 1 |
| 8 | 13 to 1 | 33 | 100 to 1 |
| 9 | 9 to 1 | 32 | 77 to 1 |
| 10 | 6½ to 1 | 31 | 63 to 1 |
| 11 | 5 to 1 | 30 | 53 to 1 |
| 12 | 4 to 1 | 29 | 43 to 1 |
| 13 | 3 to 1 | 28 | 31 to 1 |
| 14 | 2½ to 1 | 27 | 23 to 1 |
| 15 | Even | 26 | 17 to 1 |
| | | 25 | 13 to 1 |
| | | 24 | 10 to 1 |
| | | 23 | 8 to 1 |
| | | 22 | 6½ to 1 |
| | | 21 | 5 to 1 |
| | | 20 | 4 to 1 |
| | | 19 | 3½ to 1 |
| | | 18 | 3 to 1 |
| | | 17 | 2 to 1 |
| | | 16 | Even |

**Including pegging and the crib**

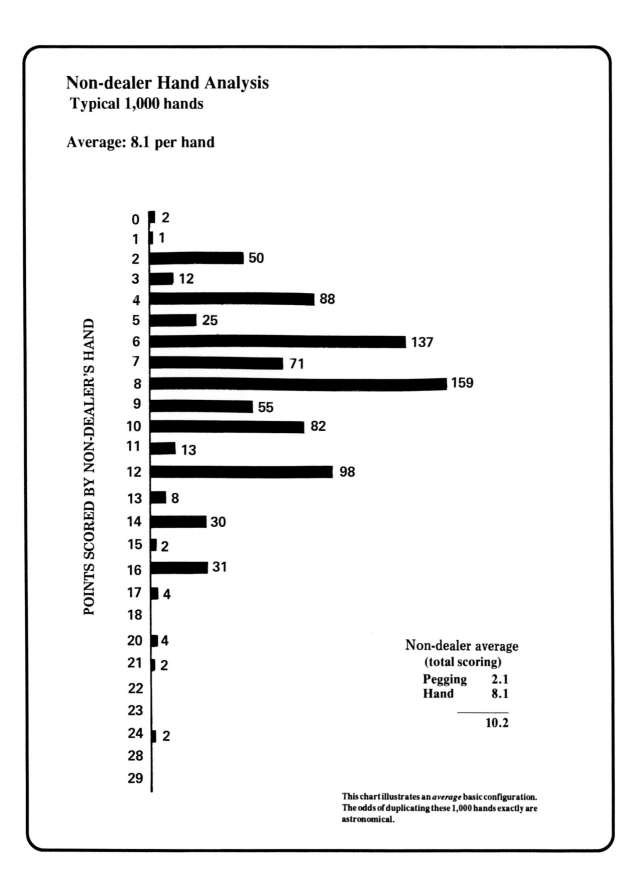

# Non-dealer Hand Analysis
## Typical 1,000 hands

**Average: 8.1 per hand**

POINTS SCORED BY NON-DEALER'S HAND

| Points | Count |
|---|---|
| 0 | 2 |
| 1 | 1 |
| 2 | 50 |
| 3 | 12 |
| 4 | 88 |
| 5 | 25 |
| 6 | 137 |
| 7 | 71 |
| 8 | 159 |
| 9 | 55 |
| 10 | 82 |
| 11 | 13 |
| 12 | 98 |
| 13 | 8 |
| 14 | 30 |
| 15 | 2 |
| 16 | 31 |
| 17 | 4 |
| 18 | |
| 20 | 4 |
| 21 | 2 |
| 22 | |
| 23 | |
| 24 | 2 |
| 28 | |
| 29 | |

Non-dealer average
(total scoring)
Pegging    2.1
Hand       8.1
———————
10.2

This chart illustrates an *average* basic configuration.
The odds of duplicating these 1,000 hands exactly are
astronomical.

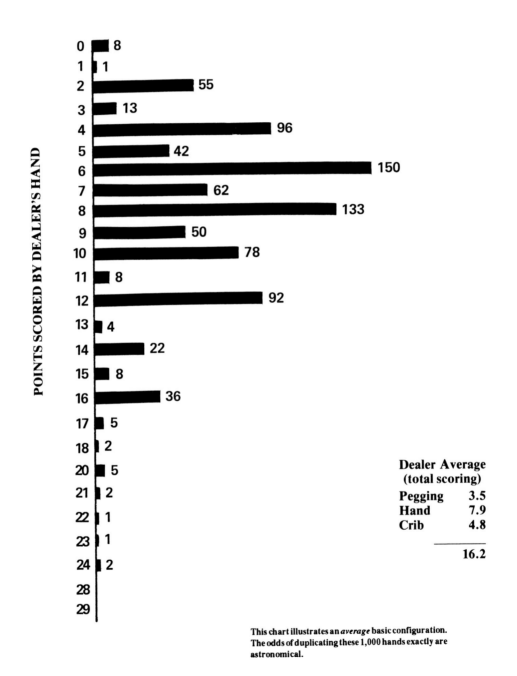

# Dealer Hand Analysis
## Typical 1,000 hands

**Average: 7.9 per hand**

**POINTS SCORED BY DEALER'S HAND**

| Points | Count |
|---|---|
| 0 | 8 |
| 1 | 1 |
| 2 | 55 |
| 3 | 13 |
| 4 | 96 |
| 5 | 42 |
| 6 | 150 |
| 7 | 62 |
| 8 | 133 |
| 9 | 50 |
| 10 | 78 |
| 11 | 8 |
| 12 | 92 |
| 13 | 4 |
| 14 | 22 |
| 15 | 8 |
| 16 | 36 |
| 17 | 5 |
| 18 | 2 |
| 20 | 5 |
| 21 | 2 |
| 22 | 1 |
| 23 | 1 |
| 24 | 2 |
| 28 | |
| 29 | |

**Dealer Average**
**(total scoring)**

| Pegging | 3.5 |
|---|---|
| Hand | 7.9 |
| Crib | 4.8 |
| | 16.2 |

This chart illustrates an *average* basic configuration.
The odds of duplicating these 1,000 hands exactly are
astronomical.

# Crib Hand Analysis
## Typical 1,000 hands

## Average: 4.8  per crib

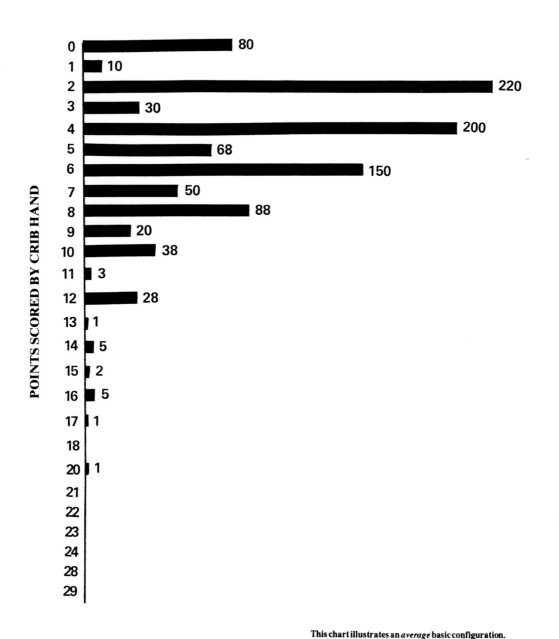

This chart illustrates an *average* basic configuration. The odds of duplicating these 1,000 hands exactly are astronomical.

## Margin of Winning Analysis
(average point margin per game)

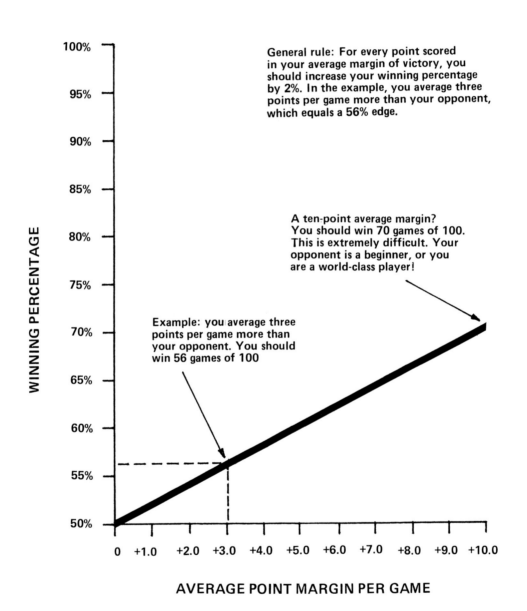

General rule: For every point scored in your average margin of victory, you should increase your winning percentage by 2%. In the example, you average three points per game more than your opponent, which equals a 56% edge.

A ten-point average margin? You should win 70 games of 100. This is extremely difficult. Your opponent is a beginner, or you are a world-class player!

Example: you average three points per game more than your opponent. You should win 56 games of 100

WINNING PERCENTAGE

AVERAGE POINT MARGIN PER GAME

## Discarding Risks

This chart illustrates the average risk of discarding to the opponent's crib. The very best discards to balk your opponent's crib is the 10-king combination (3.8 point average crib), followed by the 9-king. The third best balking combination is the 9-queen, followed by the 6-king (see chart, following page).

The worst discard combinations are the 5-5 (9.3 average crib), followed by the 7-8 (7.8 average) and the 5-jack (7.6 average). Other risky discards are the 5-6, 5-10, 5-queen, 2-3, 4-5, 5-king, 7-7, and 6-6. These combinations will average 7.0+ per crib (average).

Study this chart. In a tight game, the right discard could certainly win the game for you!

How does discarding the same suit vs. different suits affect the average? An insignificant .03...but do NOT get careless, as a matching suit discard will bite you for a flush in the crib about one time in 17.

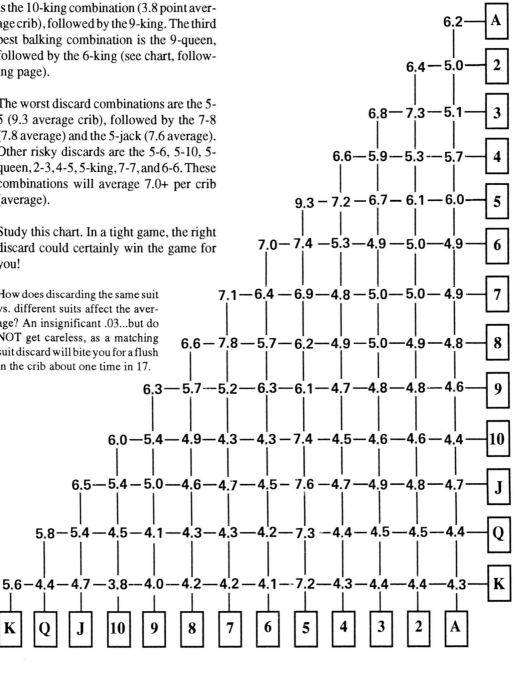

**Opponent's Crib**

| | K | Q | J | 10 | 9 | 8 | 7 | 6 | 5 | 4 | 3 | 2 | A |
|---|---|---|---|---|---|---|---|---|---|---|---|---|---|
| **A** | | | | | | | | | | | | | 6.2 |
| **2** | | | | | | | | | | | 6.4 | 5.0 | |
| **3** | | | | | | | | | | 6.8 | 7.3 | 5.1 | |
| **4** | | | | | | | | | 6.6 | 5.9 | 5.3 | 5.7 | |
| **5** | | | | | | | | 9.3 | 7.2 | 6.7 | 6.1 | 6.0 | |
| **6** | | | | | | | 7.0 | 7.4 | 5.3 | 4.9 | 5.0 | 4.9 | |
| **7** | | | | | | 7.1 | 6.4 | 6.9 | 4.8 | 5.0 | 5.0 | 4.9 | |
| **8** | | | | | 6.6 | 7.8 | 5.7 | 6.2 | 4.9 | 5.0 | 4.9 | 4.8 | |
| **9** | | | | 6.3 | 5.7 | 5.2 | 6.3 | 6.1 | 4.7 | 4.8 | 4.8 | 4.6 | |
| **10** | | | 6.0 | 5.4 | 4.9 | 4.3 | 4.3 | 7.4 | 4.5 | 4.6 | 4.6 | 4.4 | |
| **J** | | 6.5 | 5.4 | 5.0 | 4.6 | 4.7 | 4.5 | 7.6 | 4.7 | 4.9 | 4.8 | 4.7 | |
| **Q** | 5.8 | 5.4 | 4.5 | 4.1 | 4.3 | 4.3 | 4.2 | 7.3 | 4.4 | 4.5 | 4.5 | 4.4 | |
| **K** | 5.6 | 4.4 | 4.7 | 3.8 | 4.0 | 4.2 | 4.2 | 4.1 | 7.2 | 4.3 | 4.4 | 4.4 | 4.3 |

## Discarding Advantages

This chart illustrates the average advantages (and disadvantages) of discarding to your own crib. The very best discard for maximum (average) score is the 5-5 (8.6 average) followed by the 2-3 (6.9 average), the 5-jack (6.9), the 5-10 (6.6), 7-8 (6.6), and the 5-queen, 5-king combinations for 6.6 average scores.

The worst discards into your own crib are the 10-king (2.8), 9-queen (3.0), 9-king (3.1), and the 6-queen, 6-king combinations for 3.1 point average cribs.

Check the chart on the next page for values of crib discards in descending order.

And once again, if you can match your suits when discarding (without affecting your count), then do so, as one time in 17 (average) you will be rewarded with a crib flush...and a nice bonus of five points!

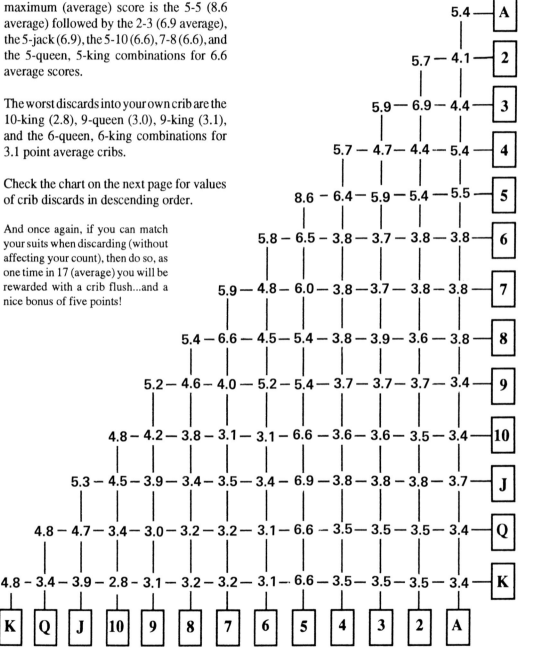

116

## Average Value of Crib Discards in Descending Order

This chart illustrates the average value of discards, in descending order, to your own crib, and to your opponent's crib.

These averages DO NOT take into account hands that will REDUCE the odds of scoring. For example, you are holding A-A-2-2-3-4. You decide to discard the A-A to your opponent's crib. The chart shows that this discard will average 6.2 (and is a fairly dangerous discard). The A-4 discard on the chart shows a 5.7 risk...a full .5 better than the A-A. However, in this case, your 2-2-3-4 cards cut the odds of a large crib, as you are holding four cards that "cut off" the odds of the aces scoring.

Another example: you are holding 6-6-7-7-8-8, and discard the 6-8 to your opponent's crib. The chart indicates a 5.7 risk with this discard, but, in reality, by holding the 6-7-7-8, you have cut the odds of the crib's scoring.

However, study this chart. In a tight pinch, when all factors are equal, knowing these averages may be the edge to pick up a tough win!

| Your Crib | | | |
|---|---|---|---|
| 5-5 = 8.6 | | 2-7 = 3.8 | |
| 2-3 = 6.9 | | 3-J = 3.8 | |
| 5-J = 6.9 | | 4-J = 3.8 | |
| 5-10 = 6.6 | | 8-10 = 3.8 | |
| 7-8 = 6.6 | | A-7 = 3.8 | |
| 5-Q = 6.6 | | 4-6 = 3.8 | |
| 5-K = 6.6 | | 2-J = 3.8 | |
| 5-6 = 6.5 | | A-8 = 3.8 | |
| 4-5 = 6.4 | | 4-7 = 3.8 | |
| 5-7 = 6.0 | | 3-6 = 3.7 | |
| 7-7 = 5.9 | | 4-9 = 3.7 | |
| 3-5 = 5.9 | | 3-9 = 3.7 | |
| 3-3 = 5.9 | | A-J = 3.7 | |
| 6-6 = 5.7 | | 2-9 = 3.7 | |
| 4-4 = 5.7 | | 3-7 = 3.7 | |
| 2-2 = 5.7 | | 2-8 = 3.6 | |
| A-5 = 5.5 | | 4-10 = 3.6 | |
| 5-8 = 5.5 | | 3-10 = 3.6 | |
| 8-8 = 5.4 | | 4-Q = 3.5 | |
| A-4 = 5.4 | | 3-K = 3.5 | |
| 2-5 = 5.4 | | 3-Q = 3.5 | |
| 5-9 = 5.4 | | 4-K = 3.5 | |
| A-A = 5.4 | | 2-10 = 3.5 | |
| J-J = 5.3 | | 2-K = 3.5 | |
| 9-9 = 5.2 | | 2-Q = 3.5 | |
| 6-9 = 5.2 | | 7-J = 3.5 | |
| 10-10 = 4.8 | | 8-J = 3.4 | |
| 6-7 = 4.8 | | A-9 = 3.4 | |
| K-K = 4.8 | | Q-K = 3.4 | |
| Q-Q = 4.8 | | A-10 = 3.4 | |
| J-Q = 4.7 | | A-Q = 3.4 | |
| 3-4 = 4.7 | | A-K = 3.4 | |
| 8-9 = 4.6 | | 6-J = 3.4 | |
| 6-8 = 4.5 | | 10-Q = 3.4 | |
| 10-J = 4.5 | | 8-K = 3.2 | |
| 2-4 = 4.4 | | 8-Q = 3.2 | |
| A-3 = 4.3 | | 7-Q = 3.2 | |
| 9-10 = 4.2 | | 7-K = 3.2 | |
| A-2 = 4.1 | | 7-10 = 3.1 | |
| 7-9 = 4.0 | | 6-10 = 3.1 | |
| 9-J = 4.0 | | 6-K = 3.1 | |
| J-K = 3.9 | | 6-Q = 3.1 | |
| 3-8 = 3.9 | | 9-K = 3.1 | |
| 2-6 = 3.8 | | 9-Q = 3.0 | |
| 4-8 = 3.8 | | 10-K = 2.8 | |
| A-6 = 3.8 | | | |

| Opponent's Crib | | | |
|---|---|---|---|
| 5-5 = 9.3 | | 8-10 = 4.9 | |
| 7-8 = 7.8 | | A-7 = 4.9 | |
| 5-J = 7.6 | | 2-8 = 4.9 | |
| 5-6 = 7.4 | | 4-8 = 4.9 | |
| 5-10 = 7.4 | | A-6 = 4.9 | |
| 5-Q = 7.3 | | 3-6 = 4.9 | |
| 2-3 = 7.3 | | 3-J = 4.9 | |
| 4-5 = 7.2 | | 2-J = 4.8 | |
| 5-K = 7.2 | | A-8 = 4.8 | |
| 7-7 = 7.1 | | 4-7 = 4.8 | |
| 6-6 = 7.0 | | 3-9 = 4.8 | |
| 5-7 = 6.9 | | 2-9 = 4.7 | |
| 3-3 = 6.8 | | J-K = 4.7 | |
| 3-5 = 6.7 | | 4-J = 4.7 | |
| 4-4 = 6.6 | | A-J = 4.7 | |
| 8-8 = 6.6 | | 4-9 = 4.7 | |
| J-J = 6.5 | | 7-J = 4.6 | |
| 2-2 = 6.4 | | A-9 = 4.6 | |
| 6-7 = 6.3 | | 3-10 = 4.6 | |
| 9-9 = 6.3 | | 2-10 = 4.6 | |
| 6-9 = 6.3 | | 8-J = 4.5 | |
| 5-8 = 6.2 | | 6-J = 4.5 | |
| A-A = 6.2 | | 3-Q = 4.5 | |
| 2-5 = 6.1 | | 2-Q = 4.5 | |
| 5-9 = 6.1 | | 10-Q = 4.5 | |
| A-5 = 6.0 | | 4-10 = 4.5 | |
| 10-10 = 6.0 | | 3-K = 4.4 | |
| 3-4 = 5.9 | | A-10 = 4.4 | |
| Q-Q = 5.8 | | 2-K = 4.4 | |
| A-4 = 5.7 | | 4-Q = 4.4 | |
| 6-8 = 5.7 | | Q-K = 4.4 | |
| 8-9 = 5.7 | | A-Q = 4.4 | |
| K-K = 5.6 | | 7-10 = 4.3 | |
| 10-J = 5.4 | | 4-K = 4.3 | |
| 9-10 = 5.4 | | 7-Q = 4.3 | |
| J-Q = 5.4 | | 8-Q = 4.3 | |
| 4-6 = 5.3 | | 6-10 = 4.3 | |
| 2-4 = 5.3 | | A-K = 4.3 | |
| 7-9 = 5.2 | | 7-K = 4.2 | |
| A-3 = 5.1 | | 6-Q = 4.2 | |
| A-2 = 5.0 | | 8-K = 4.2 | |
| 3-7 = 5.0 | | 6-K = 4.1 | |
| 2-7 = 5.0 | | 9-Q = 4.1 | |
| 2-6 = 5.0 | | 9-K = 4.0 | |
| 9-J = 5.0 | | 10-K = 3.8 | |
| 3-8 = 4.9 | | | |

# Tournament Cribbage

American Cribbage Congress
Tournament Rules & Guidelines
National Ratings
Independent Tournaments

## Tournament Cribbage

Tournament cribbage! Now that you have studied the preceding chapters and have a feel for the entire game, you should give tournament cribbage a try. If you truly want to know how you rank among other players, tournament play will quickly let you know.

But don't let one tournament be your guideline. You must play a number of times...and you must keep records. The Law of Averages over a long term should be your guideline. Anyone can have a temporary run of superior cards...or a temporary run of inferior cards. But, over time, these anomolies will even out and you will get an average...an average on the positive side of the ledger if you have done your homework, practiced the "Twenty-Six" Theory, and know when to "play on" and when to "play off" to acheive your board position. And, of course, know how (and when) to run trap plays, peg for advantage, discard properly, and play a sound, consistent, all-around game.

And, of course, don't let winning or losing be the sole factor in deciding if you should compete or not. The social aspect of the game cannot be overlooked. The friends you will make, and the thrill of competing head-to-head on a regular basis with the best in the nation make cribbage that much more exciting.

Tournament players, after a time, will begin sharing their homes to fellow tournament travelers, and life-long friendships will be made. Cribbage players are a unique group, and their sociability are legend. After a trial tournament or two, many players will make cribbage their primary avocation, and will travel hundreds of miles to pursue "the game!"

## American Cribbage Congress

The best cribbage organization in America is the American Cribbage Congress. This organization was founded in 1979, and has enjoyed steady growth since. Their tournament concept, complete with a rating system for players nationwide, has been well accepted.

In 1992, this organization boasts some 6,600 members, and are held together nationally by a *Cribbage World* trade publication. This monthly magazine lists sanctioned tournaments in a "Tournament Trail" section, giving players the name of tournaments, dates played, entry fees, and other pertinent information. For the serious player who enjoys spirited competition, this is the ultimate cribbage experience. Even players who play on a more casual basis, an occasional tournament is a very enjoyable, social experience.

The American Cribbage Congress's rating system is based on only sanctioned tournaments, with a numerical system based on the number of participants, with the top 12 1/2% (1 in 8) finishers earning Master Rating Points. The Congress's system awards players Master, Grand Master, and Life Master ratings. In addition, the top 10 players are awarded All-American status on a yearly basis. The Congress directly conducts a Grand National event yearly, rotating between three regions of the country (Eastern, Central, and Western), and a yearly Joseph Petrus Wergin/ACC Open that has been drawing huge crowds of peggers to Reno, Nevada in January or February. For example, in 1992, some 842 peggers were on hand...with the winner receiving a whopping $10,000.

*To Join the American Cribbage Congress:*
1993 membership fees: $7 single, $8 married couple.
Write to
**DeLynn Colvert, PO Box 5604, Missoula, MT 59806**
**...or call 1-800-WE PEG 29 for information**

# Tournament Rules and Guidelines

The American Cribbage Congress's sanctioned tournaments are governed by cribbage's basic rules. However, some special rules do apply to tournaments.

For example, sanctioned tournaments require that every player **MUST cut the deck after the dealer has shuffled.** Then the cards are dealt. This rule is an obvious necessity, since many players are complete strangers, and a "mechanic" who can deal from the bottom of the deck, or even worse, may come along. However, in my long tournament experiences, I have never suspected anyone of this devious practice. But, I have seen a few players who will "pack wood." This overpegging is an art form with a handful of players, and they will skillfully employ this tactic when playing players who are inattentive. elderly, or on the gullible side. But, once again, this is a rarity among cribbage players...who are renowned for their sociabilty and fair play. If you suspect your opponent of devious shuffling, you are entitled to re-shuffle the pack when offered the cut. However, the dealer is entitled to the last shuffle before cutting for deal.

Other tournament rules that are unique to sanctioned play are:

**Overpegging.** If points are overpegged, and your opppponent catches the overpeg, you are required to move your peg backwards to the correct hole. Your opponent then pegs the amount of overpeg. For example, you call "ten" but peg 15. This is a 5-point penalty. However, if you catch the mistake, you can quickly correct your pegs to the correct hole (no penalty).

**Underpegging.** If you peg short, and let go of your peg, you CANNOT advance the peg upon discovering the mistake.

**Falsely claiming the game.** If you falsely claim the game by pegging out with insufficient count, and your opponent catches the error, you are penalized 15 holes backward from the hole you have earned, and your opponent is awarded, in addition to the backward 15-hole penalty, the amount of overpeg. For example, you call "ten" and claim the game (needing 10 to win, being in hole 111) . But your count was only six, and your opponent catches the mistake. You must go back to hole 117, and THEN take a 15-point penalty backwards. In addition, your opponent pegs a 4-point overpeg penalty.

**Claiming the game.** One of the most common mistakes a new tournament player will make is not claiming the game. You must put your peg in the winner's hole and claim the game, otherwise, the game continues. This rule has caused consternation among tournament players. The rule is difficult to enforce, and when a judge is called to enforce the rule, hard feelings are created. The American Cribbage Congress has wrestled with this rule, with a variety of solutions. To avoid any controversy, **ALWAYS PEG OUT AND CLAIM THE GAME!**

**Misdealing.** A variety of errors can occur when dealing. You can deal yourself five cards, you opponent seven, etc. The American Cribbage Congress has published a rule book that covers all situations when misdealing, or mis-discarding. For example, too may cards are dealt (seven to each player). If the mistake is discovered before the starter card is turned, you simply re-deal. However, if the starter card is turned, play stops at time of discovery. Both hands are dead and the dealer counts the crib. On the other hand, if only five cards are dealt, and the mistake is discovered before the starter card is turned, the cards are re-dealt. After the starter card is turned and the short-hand discovery is made, play continues and the short hands (and crib) are counted in the proper order. There are many possible misdealing situations, and the official rule book clarifies the solutions. Caution. If you have been dealt an incorrect hand (too many or too few), you **MUST show your opponent this incorrect hand.** If you do not (and put the hand on top of the deck without confirming the error by showing your opponent), you will be assessed a backward penalty of 10 points (or enough to put your pegs off the board if the game has just begun).

**Exposing a card or cards when dealing.** If the dealer exposes a card (or cards) while dealing, they are simply picked up, reshuffled and redealt.

**Face up card in pack.** If a card is found face up in the deck, they cards are reshuffled and redealt.

**Cut card is face up.** Turn this card over, reshuffle the pack (keeping your hands) and re-cut.

**Imperfect pack.** If a deck is found to have a defective card, or obvious visual defect, a new deck shall be put into play. If, however, the cards have been picked up by either player, the hand is played, **then** a new deck is put into play.

**Discarding to the crib.** Cards placed in a crib cannot be picked up and re-evaluated, unless, prior to turning the starter card, one player (only) has discarded to the wrong side. That player is permitted to retrieve his cards and re-evaluate the discard. Once both players have discarded to the crib on the wrong side, and one player catches the mistake, all four cards are simply moved to the correct side. But, once the starter card has been turned, and each player has played one card, then the crib stays where placed. The next crib hand alternates, however.

**Incorrect announcement when pegging.** If a player incorrectly announces the count when pegging, the opponent may correct the count, or use the incorrect count to his or her advantage. Once a card has been called and played, an incorrect count cannot be corrected, and play continues.

**Pegging in the wrong direction.** One of the most severe mistakes a player can make is pegging in the wrong direction. Once a peg is released, the pegs remain where placed.

**Picking up the front peg.** If a player inadvertently picks up his front peg, and clears the hole, this peg now becomes the back peg. The latest score is then pegged from the back peg.

**Pegging with opponent's pegs.** If you peg forward with your opponent's pegs, you have forfeited your pegs and your opponent keeps them. If the error is discovered before releasing the peg, then the peg is returned to the original hole, and the correct score is pegged with your own pegs. However, for illegally touching your opponent's peg, you are assessed a two-point penalty.

**Moving opponent's pegs backwards.** This is another severe penalty. If you move your opponent's pegs backwards, they are replaced in the proper hole, and you forfeit the points of the play, hand, or crib in question.

**Recording your score in opponent's track.** If you peg your points in your opponent's track, you may correct the peg to your own track. No penalty.

**Exposing your cards when counting (or when pegging).** Cards shall be fully exposed when counting or pegging.

**Starter card.** The starter card must remain segregated from the hand (or crib) at all times. If this card is intermingled with a hand (or crib), a two-point penalty is assessed, and the card is then segregated properly. If there is disagreement concerning this starter card, summon a judge.

**Mixing a hand with the crib.** If a hand and crib are mixed before it is counted and scored, and before the opponent has confirmed the count, the player forfeits the count of the hand. If the crib is involved, and the dealer commits the offense, the dealer forfeits the crib count also. If the nondealer mixes the dealer's cards, the dealer is permitted to retrieve and reconstruct the hand and crib. The non-dealer is penalized two points. If agreement cannot be reached, summon a judge.

**Assistance in counting.** No aid from any sort can be given to a player, including charts, notes, or from any spectator.

**Muggins.** Muggins is the only optional rule in tournament play. Only a handful of tournaments employ the muggins rule (and, usually these are the larger, more prestigious tournaments, such as the American Cribbage Congress's "Tournament of Champions." This tournament is by invite only). For a complete description of this rule, obtain a copy of the ACC's rule book. In general, for every point missed by your opponent, you score the missed points by announcing "muggins" and taking the missed points.

# How Organized Cribbage Began in the USA

Cribbage was invented by Sir John Suckling in the early 1600's, and in the ensuing 375 years or so, cribbage tournaments have been played...some small and some large. But as for organized play, only a few local clubs in forgotten, unrecorded places have had tournament play. Cribbage, for the first 350 years, was primarily a family, social game (as were most card games).

One of the earliest tournaments recorded was organized by Raymond "Rasty" Rasmussen at the Iowa State Fair in 1932...and he continued this Iowa State Fair tournament for some 50 years. He retired from his tournament in 1982 at the age of 80, and in 1987 was enshrined in the Cribbage Hall of Fame for his dedication to the Grand Old Game.

Another "oldie" was the YMCA Championship, played in Wilmington, NC in 1969.

But the "Granddaddy" of tournament play, as we know it today, was Nick Pond's National Open that was organized in 1974. Pond spared no effort to make this a first-class event, and it continues today with players from throughout the United States and Canada converging on Raleigh, NC, for their annual cribbage pilgrimage.

Out west in California in the winter of 1972, Everett Bey, and some local Chamber of Commerce executives in Quincy, CA, met at the Plumas Club to discuss a "County Cribbage Championship." After a few drinks, they decided on a "State Championship." But, in winding down the evening, they settled on a "World Championship!" And so the First Annual World Cribbage Championship was spawned, played in May 1972, and continues its run today. This tournament was the forerunner of many California tournaments...and it earned "Ev" Bey the office of Vice President in the American Cribbage Congress, and the honor of being elected to the Cribbage Hall of Fame. Among early California tournaments was the First Kiwanis Championship, organized by Lou DeLu in Cupertino, CA in June of 1979. Other notable cribbage organizers were Mary and Dick Cornwell, Sunnyvale, CA. They held the first California Championships in the early 1980's.

Up in the Northwest, Rob Palmer, Baker City, Oregon, began the Northwest Open in the spring of 1978. And from this Oregon tournament, Joe Nelson, a cribbage-board maker in Prineville, OR, began his Oregon State Championships. Nelson's tournaments have drawn large crowds (well over 300 players) and his skill as a board maker (for trophies) is renowned throughout the Northwest.

In Idaho, Roy Carlson, Wallace, organized the first Idaho Championship matches, beginning in October 1981.

Back in the midwest, Joseph Petrus Wergin, Madison, WI, was busy writing books on skat, euchre, and cribbage, and was skilled in running skat tournaments. In 1979, while attending the National Open in Raleigh, NC, he sat down at an informal breakfast with National Open Director Nick Pond, Jim Arblaster, and other notable cribbage buffs from around the nation. This August 6, 1979 meeting spawned the American Cribbage Congress. Wergin went back to Wisconsin, and in February 1980, the World Masters Classic was played in Madison. This began a rapid expansion of tournaments in the midwest. The M&M Open, under Pete Danielson (Marinette, WI), and the MGM in Green Bay (Tom Gallagher, Jerry Lemke, and Bob Miller) are among the earliest tournaments in that area.

Meanwhile, in New England, Joe Andrews organized the 1st New Hampshire Open, played in Nashua in October 1981. Shortly thereafter, George Bickford played the first New England Open in West Springfield, Massachusetts in November 1981. John Chambers, Providence, RI, organized the Rhode Island Cribbage League in the early 1980's, which grew rapidly into a sizeable group of peggers. From this beginning, organized cribbage rapidly grew in the New England area, and, in the early 1990's is one of cribbage's "hot beds."

Meanwhile, in Montana, DeLynn Colvert wrote a book "Play Winning Cribbage" and began selling by mail order throughout the United States. A buyer in Connecticut wrote Colvert about the new American Cribbage Congress, and he quickly joined. Shortly thereafter, the first Montana tournaments were organized, culminating in the Grand National, played in Missoula in September, 1993. Other Montana tournaments began play in 1985.

In Colordo, Dick Graham and Iris Fuller began hosting tournaments in 1980 and 1981, and Denver hosted the 4th Annual Grand National in September 1985. Graham also was appointed Director of the first two

"Tournament of Champion" events that were played at the Riviera Casino, Las Vegas, Nevada, November, 1983 and December, 1984. This tournament is by invitation only, and is now played in Reno, Nevada.

As organized cribbage enters its third decade, the growth has been steady nationwide...especially in the New England, Washington, Oregon, and California areas. The following map graphically shows the growth of organized cribbage in the United States:

## Cribbage World Publication

The American Cribbage Congress mails a monthly *Cribbage World* publication to all members, keeping the membership informed about cribbage events nationwide. A complete listing of sanctioned tournaments is included monthly telling players when, where, and entry fee information. Another listing is Master Points earned by players in sanctioned tournaments, listed by regions (Western, Central, Eastern). Tournament results are compiled and published, giving the top finishers in all sanctioned events.

The American Cribbage Congress is a non-profit organization, with much volunteer work to keep the organization humming. One of the major jobs is publishing *Cribbage World*...and I have the honor of being the fourth editor of this trade magazine. Although entailing an enormous amount of work, it is an exciting, rewarding experience, as I have had the inside track on players nationwide, get first-hand information about tournament play, and all the "fun" vignettes about players nationwide.

I hope these tidbits of information about the American Cribbage Congress will motivate you to join...as I want to see you "on the cribbage trail!"

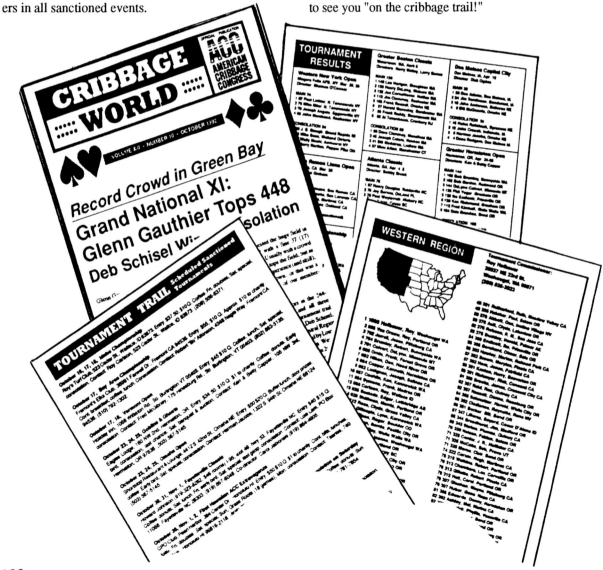

# *The Best of Cribbage World ...*

In March of 1990, I volunteered to be the 4th editor of *Cribbage World*, the American Cribbage Congress's official trade magazine. Despite the mountains of work compiling tournament winners, Master Point lists, and the myriad other chores related to publishing and mailing, the work has been most enjoyable.

The most enjoyable of all, however, is having a first hand look at all the odd happenings to players on the cribbage trail. "Old Man Murphy" is hard at work when it comes to cribbage players. I simply can't resist passing a few of these vignettes on to you. So, with approval from the American Cribbage Congress, here is the best of *Cribbage World!*

## Faux Pas at Awards Ceremony

At the recent Awards ceremony at Green Bay's Grand National, some 72 awards were made, in addition to Grass Roots awards.

All went well until the All-American awards were presented. Scott Kooistra and Joan Rein were expertly presenting the top ten with their awards. That is, until National Champion Phyllis Schmidt was on the agenda. At that time. Joan demanded the mike, as she wanted the honor of presenting the award to the first woman to ever earn the national title.

After a glowing introduction, Joan continued..."and during the 1992 season Phyllis accumulated some 1,442 POUNDS...oops! After much hooting and hollering by the audience, she continued..."I mean 1,442 MASTER POINTS!"

Shortly thereafter, Joan surrendered the mike to MC Martha Fingleton, and she mollified the situation by adding that Phyllis didn't even weigh 1,442 OUNCES!

And so ended a very enjoyable banquet and awards ceremony.

## Play the Exact Game Twice? Don't Bet on it!

How many different ways can an ordinary deck of 52 cards be arranged? Would you believe 80,658,175,170,943,878,571,660,636,856,403,766,975,289,505,440,883,277,824,000,000,000,000 possible permutations! Could this be the reason cribbage (and other card games) are so fascinating? You will never in a hundred lifetimes play the same game twice! Or at least, don't bet on it!

## John Jantos Doesn't Need His Pegs

John Jantos lost his pegs in a California tournament recently...and no one returned them (not yet). However, in Raleigh, John scored a 28-hand...with stock pegs! Who needs those fancy pegs, anyway!

## BUMPER STICKERS

127

# SONDERICKER TOPS 826
## Ken Richmond Captures TOC
**Richard Nielsen, Bill Seymour Take Consolations**

> This cribbage tournament was the largest in the history of the game. Played at the Sands Casino, Reno, Nevada, January 31, February 1, & 2, 1992, the event drew some 826 peggers from the USA and Canada.

Life Master Warren Sondericker, Greenfield, WI has added new laurels to his many cribbage exploits by winning the record-setting American Cribbage Congress Open in Reno February 2. Warren bested a record field of 826 peggers, easily topping last year's 736. His final match was with slick-pegging Bill Medeiros, South Easton, MA. Leading 3-2 in the best of seven match, Warren cut the jack of diamonds to peg out and win his fourth game and the match 4-2.

With the record crowd came record prizes...and Sondericker picked up a nifty $10,000 for the championship, while Medeiros pocketed another $6,000 for his second place finish.

Reno has been very kind to Sondericker, as he also won in 1987, besting a then-record crowd of 454, edging Rex Reid of nearby Quincy, CA for that title.

Don Hilton, Hood River, OR finished 3rd and picked up a sizeable $3,600, while professor Russell Adams, Minneapolis, MN took 4th and $2,800.

Idaho's Roy Carlson (tournament director of Idaho's October championships) finished 5th ($2,350), Don Abbott, Incline Village, NV took 6th ($1,950), Hall of Famer Bob Madsen took home $1,600 for a 7th place finish, and Morris Schiffman, Portland, OR took home $1,325 for his 8th place finish.

And the prize money for the "Q" pools were sizeable as well...as Richard Harper, Ashland, OR, burned up the track in the qualifying round and posted a 41-GP score to take home the top "Q" prize of $1,750.

The marquee outside the Sands Casino proclaimed to the world that this was "The World's Largest Cribbage Tournament" and that held true for the ACC Open's consolation event as well, as 644 peggers signed on for a second chance at the richest tournament ever.

Richard Nielsen, Omaha, NE, came up roses by edging Canadian Egon Koch (Surrey, BC) for the title. Nielsen pocketed $3,000 for the largest consolation prize ever...and Koch took home $2,130 for 2nd. Jim Fabian, Naperville, ILL edged closer to his Grand Master rating by finishing 3rd ($1,400) and Master pegger Dick Graham (Colorado's premier tournament director) finished 4th and pocketed a cool $1,000.

Karen Trojan, New Brighton, MN scored a super 21 Game Points in the 9/game qualifying round to nail the top "Q" prize of $820. (See story about Karen, this issue).

Other highlights of this record-breaking tournament include Floyd "Al" Whitsett's (Sparks, NV) 29-hand, and at least three ACC members earned their Master rating. They are Ray Meade, Las Vegas, NV; Ray Van Orsow, Portland, OR; and Roy Banducci, Arroyo Grande, CA. Twenty-eight hands? Too many to count.

## Tournament of Champions
Ken Richmond, Portland's other king of cribbage (Ray Van Orsow is the other) walked away with the championship of the by-invite-only Tournament of Champions. This meet also set a new standard for numbers of peggers...drawing some 330, easily beating last year's then-record 306. Richmond pocketed a record $6,100 for this event (but NO Master Points). The few Canadians who played in this three-day cribbage fest showed very well, indeed, as George Saari, Kamloops, BC, took 2nd and a sizeable $4,650. Master pegger Luis Lizarribar, Ballwin, MO, continued his winning ways by taking 3rd ($3,550), and Patrick Barrett, Wisconsin Rapids, WI, took 4th and $2,750. Patrick had a horrible run of cards the next day in the ACC Open...but he was still smiling!

Stuart Stromberg. West Springfield, MA, took top honors in the "Q" and walked away with $1,325...but this "top 25" player could

have used some Master Points for his fine qualifying card to move up a notch or two...but in this by-invitation-only meet, NO Master Points are awarded.

Some 202 peggers signed on for the consolation TOC. Master pegger Bill Seymour, Warwick, RI took home the title and $2,065. Jim Hartung, Richland, WA is no stranger to high finishes as he has consistently walked away with the Grass Roots prizes in the Tri-Cities (WA) and, once again, finished a lofty 2nd, picking up $1,600. Jim Morelan, a Master pegger from Little Canada, MN took 3rd, while Dave Stratford, Napa, CA took 4th.

Tournament directors Joan Rein (TOC), along with Martha Fingleton, Bob McCabe, Scott Kooistra, and Warren Sondericker all did a superb job of managing the huge crowds, and play went smoothly in all events. Jeff Shimp did a wonderful job with his judging crew...and of course the Sand's Barbara Woodward managed the entire weekend with her usual expertise...and all the 826 players had all the coffee and danish they wanted! If the crowds keep increasing, the Sands may have to build on once again, as a rumor has it they can only accomodate about 950 players.

And to all the 826 players who attended this meet...you may all write to the Guiness Book of Records! This was, indeed, the largest cribbage tournament in the history of the game!

## Hot Tip! How to Beat Eldon Schwilke

Eldon Schwilke, Spokane, WA, let the cat out of the bag! He recently told your editor that if he even gets a wiff of an onion, he passes out! So if you are losing to Eldon (and that happens much too often)...whip out your onion!

## Damned Sea Gull

Rollie Heath, Cloverdale, OR, won his local club cribbage championship and at the awards ceremony discovered he had won a wooden hand-painted sea gull.

Rollie commented to 2nd place winner Bernie Nelson (Pacific City, OR) that he thought the sea gull was ugly...and he had no use for it. Bernie, who had won a $20 roll of quarters agreed to trade prizes as he runs a sporting goods store...and perhaps he could sell the sea gull.

Bernie puts a $40 price tag on the sea gull, but, alas, it languishes for months unsold.

Then one day, one of Rollie's fellow school teachers comes to Bernie's store looking for a retirement gift for Rollie. Bernie says that Rollie is a collector of sea gulls, and he makes the sale.

Needless to say, the look of amazement on Rollie's face when he opened his retirement gift was one for the books!

Perhaps Rollie can drill holes in the sea gull and make a cribbage board.

## 94 Years Old?

A reliable source informed Cribbage World that at his present pace, Rollie Heath, Lincoln City, OR, will be 94 years old when he earns his Master rating!

Readers may recall that Rollie was the recipient of an unwanted wooden sea gull for his retirement gift...and, perhaps when he turns 94 and earns his Master award, there wont be space for the award on his walls as they will probably be covered with wooden sea gulls.

## Can You Top This?

Ike Endicott, Prineville, OR and DeLynn Colvert, Missoula, MT cut for the deal to begin a qualifying-round game. Both players cut threes. Reshuffle, recut...again 2 threes. Reshuffle, recut...this time 2 nines. Reshuffle, recut...this time 2 dueces. Four consecutive ties...83,521 to 1 odds. Cribbage World is standing by awaiting word of five consecutive ties.

## Record Waxing!

Randy Braukmann, Hillsboro, OR suffered a record drubbing at the recent Montana Championship. He lost by 96 points!

His opponent was Fritz DelPlanche, Cornelius, OR. Fritz said Randy did NOT peg backwards...he simply failed to draw a hand of any kind, while Fritz picked up 24's, 20's, and 16's at every turn.

Cribbage World will publish any game that tops this (no backwards pegging, please)...provided the skunkee doesn't object. The skunker may report the game, and keep his victim's name anonymous.

## Damned Sticky Pegs!

Jeanne Hofbauer, Washougal, WA, was involved in a very close game at the recent Cascade Classic VII. Her opponent needed but a few pegs to win, and grabbed the front peg to score his hand. Jeanne held her breath...for if he picked up his front peg, it would become his back peg, and she would surely win the game!

Alas, the peg stuck in the hole. It stuck so tightly that the board was raised from the table. But before it came unstuck, he realized he had the front peg, and gently set the board down, and then pegged with the proper peg.

Jeanne was on a bad roll...and this was the "tap" shot!

## Starched Underwear?

Pearl Cannon, Missoula, MT rarely plays in sanctioned competition, but she gave it a try at the recent Montana Open...and she was top qualifier in the 76-pegger consolation.

After winning her first playoff match, she was paired against her son, John. With but 26 to go to win the match, she overpegged two points and John took the two point penalty. Luck would have it, John pegged three with his last card on the next deal to win the match. Without the penalty, Pearl would have won.

A reliable source told *Cribbage World* that Pearl was overheard muttering to herself when she left the table "that son of mine is gonna get starched underwear!"

## Paddle Wheel Queen Sinks, But Not to Worry

Grand National Director Harry Stoops reports that the Paddle Wheel Queen, contracted for the Grand National Awards Banquet, has sued for Chapter 7 bankruptcy, and has "sunk," along with Harry's $350 deposit.

But not to worry, Harry has contracted with the Jungle Queen to take over the cruise and Awards Banquet. This vessel seats 180, so first come, first serve.

The trip consists of a trip up the New River in Fort Lauderdale, a meal of barbeque ribs, chicken, and shrimp...all the while gazing on palatial estates and other Florida scenery. Three cocktails are included, with a cash bar to follow.

Harry reports that it should be a fantastic Saturday night...so sign up early!

## Walrus Tusk Cribbage Board Sells for $1,700

At the recent Willis Henry auction (site unknown by CW), an ivory walrus tusk with two carved mating walrus' hand and seal, scrimshaw walrus with three seals, carved in relief and sterling inlay (16" long) sold for $1,700!

If any of our ACC members are interested in collecting (or selling) cribbage boards, CW suggests you join the Cribbage Board Collectors Society. Send your name and address, with $8 dues (year begins April 1) to:

Bette L. Bemis
Box 170
Carolina, RI 02812

The membership includes a quarterly newsletter "Members of the Board."

## Two 29's Within 5 Minutes!

In the "early bird" of the recent Hawkeye Classic, played in Des Moines, Iowa, TWO 29 HANDS WERE SCORED WITHIN 5 MINUTES! The first was scored by Kay Griffin, Des Moines, and the second by Lew Foss of Minneapolis.

Kay and Lew are just a little too fast on the draw. The next day these perfect hands would have been worth a cool $100! And membership in our ACC's exclusive "29 Club."

## Antique Boards, Anyone?

Milton Wasby, Belmont, MA, wrote Cribbage World recently describing a very interesting cribbage board collection. Anyone who would like to correspond with Milton concerning his collection:

Milton C. Wasby
35 Pequossette Road
Belmont, MA 02178

Another interesting letter recently received by Cribbage World from Bette Bemis (Bette's Cribb...ad in this issue) describes the trials and tribulations of the cribbage board collector.

We quote from her letter...

"I met an antique dealer last year who has a board collection (less than 100), and he told me a funny story about his methods of collecting them. He looks for them at all the shows where he sets up, usually getting them for a steal because dealers want to get rid of them. At one show, a dealer had an exceptional one on her table, and he knew he had to own it. He picked it up, slowly turned it over, and finally asked what the holes were for. She looked him dead in the eye, and without hesitation, responded that they were there so that they would match all the other boards he had in his collection. He didn't remember ever seeing her at previous shows, but she had seem him and knew about his collection. He said that it was one of his most embarrassing moments!"

## April Quiz

What famous pegger has this license plate?

Clue: This ACC member won the 1984 California Championship in San Jose, CA.

## April Quiz Solution

This license plate has been seen throughout the Western United States (and as far East as Minneapolis)...and is the property of Milo Roinstad, a retired machinist who is ranked 124 in the USA (lifetime). His hometown is Missoula, Montana.

## Atta Way, Mom!

Cribbage World believes Warren Sondericker, winner of the 1992 ACC Open (the largest cribbage tournament in history) has earned the right to have his favorite cribbage story published.

Warren Sondericker plays his cribbage out of Milwaukee...and one of his chief competitors is Jim McManus. Warren is one of seven Life Masters, and Jim is just a notch behind and has his Grand Master rating. When these two competitors play head to head, the stakes are usually "10-20" ($10 for a win, $20 for a skunk). And, of course, the money goes one way, then the other, depending on the luck of the draw, since they are fairly evenly matched.

One evening Warren invited his mother to play. Mrs. Sondericker plays very little, but she agreed to spend the evening doing a little pegging. Luck would have it that she drew Grand Master McManus for a game.

McManus taps Warren on the shoulder and asks "10-20 on your mother?" Warren takes a quick double take, and being a little irritated about the apparent unfair situation, retorts "No...let's make it 20-40!"

To make a long story short (and the game was short!), Mrs. Sondericker couldn't miss! Hand after hand she waxed poor Jim. When the smoke had cleared, Jim found himself double-skunked by 63 holes! And Warren had his $40.

Atta way, Mom!

## 28-Hands a Pox in Northfield

Four players scored 28-hands in the Jesse James Open in Northfield, MN, November 6...and they all lost the game!

Cribbage World has been asked NOT to print their names.

# Ken Capper First in Raleigh

...to sign up for the consolation!

## Did Duane Toll Say This?

In his drive to win the MGM championship, Duane Toll had beaten 4 men to reach the 9-16 bracket...and now he thought he had drawn a woman for his next match. He was overheard saying: "Geez, now I have to play a woman, I'm going to have to start thinking unorthodox..."

When questioned by Joan Rein, ACC's secretary, and your editor, he denied making the statement. However, lucky for Duane, the match was in error, and he continued his march to the title, waxing his fellow male opponents.

## A Hex on Grand Nationals?

Last year's Grand National in Fort Lauderdale, FL, had a site cancellation due to hotel renovations, and a bankruptcy of a chartered cruise ship, that caused director Harry Stoops much consternation.

This year's Grand National site...the Midway Motor Inn...had a $200,000 fire just three days before the tourney, much to the consternation of directors Gallagher, Lembke, and Miller. However, a massive cleanup effort on short notice kept the disruption to a minimum. Most players were unaware that a fire had occurred, as that wing of the facility was closed off.

## Treed Mountain Lion Observes Cribbage Game

Ray Baenen and Don Clark have an unusual sport out in Libby, Montana. They have a couple of hound dogs and they hunt mountain lions.

Recently they had their hounds out on a practice run, and since hunting lions was out of season, they took along their cameras just in case they treed any lions.

Luck would have it, they did, indeed, run across a mountain lion, and their hounds promptly ran the lion up a tree. After taking a few photos, they sat down...and brought out a cribbage board from their knapsack and proceeded to play a game. With the hounds baying, the lion watching, the game was on! Cribbage is not the best of spectator sports. Do you suppose the mountain lion enjoyed the game?

## Vignettes from Fort Lauderdale

Harvey Honeycutt, 1989's Grand National Champion from Beatty, OR, was overheard saying (after a bad day on the boards): "I've made a lot of mistakes this weekend...but my biggest mistake was coming to Florida!" Harvey was just kidding, of course, and is one of the northwest's best sports, win or lose!

All-American John Schuch, New London, CT counted an unusual four aces while playing Sylvia Hornbeck, Washougal, WA. Taken aback, Sylvia carefully picks up the four aces and places them one at a time in different locations in the pack to ensure they are well mixed, and shuffles for the next deal. Lo and behold, John plays four aces AGAIN the very next deal! If John can pull that trick with FIVES, he will, indeed, be unbeatable!

## Grand National's Hard Luck Story

The hard luck story deemed worst (or best) at the Grand National in Green Bay was one relayed by Pamela Ehrich, Denver, CO. Needing a skunk win to keep her hopes alive, it appeared a certainty. She needed but 7 points with first count to skunk her opponent by a whopping 57 points. Alas, she scored 5 and pegged one, ending in the stink hole. Meanwhile, her opponent held a 4-4-5-5, and a 6 was cut. The crib held a 2-7-7-8. NO SKUNK!

## *Cupid Calls . . . .*

We travel widely, just we two,
To play some cribbage and have a few.
Fame nor fortune will we attain,
Fun and friendship, that's our gain.
At every tournament we attend,
We always meet another cribbage friend.
If the creditors knock when our money runs out,
We'll not blame cribbage - we will shout.
We're making the best of this lifes journey,
With long distance friends and a cribbage tourney!

To prove how neat this game can be -
Twas at a tourney that she met me.
That's how Shirley & Arnie became "We"!

*Arnie & Shirley Schill*
*Helena, MT*

## Oops...Don't Be Late!

In the Last Roundup in Raleigh, some 154 players sat down to begin play. Oops...only 153 were present, so President Joe Wergin volunteered to take the card of the missing player. After some 20 minutes, the missing player showed up.

"Here I am" he said to Joe.

Joe continued playing. After an awkward moment, Joe turned around and asked: "Did you get into the Q-pool?"

"Yes, I did" came the reply.

"Thank You" answered Joe and then continued his game.

Oops...don't be late!

## First Tourney a Tough One

Ken Larsen's first tourney was a tough one. Playing in the 17th Annual National Open, Ken had four consecutive tough draws. Two Life Masters (Colvert, Kooistra), and two Grand Masters (Bernard, Jarrell). However, only Kooistra survived a licking. Way to go, Ken!

## Bob Madsen In Thick Of Things in Yankton

Bob Madsen, Chicago's member of the Cribbage Hall of Fame, was in the thick of the action at the recent Lewis & Clark Open in Yankton, SD.

First, he dealt John Hansen, Irene, SD, his first ever 29-hand in the Friday night "early bird" event.

In the main event, he resorted to a little trickery. Some chewing gum had stuck to his teeth, and in removing the chewing gum, he inadvertently put some gum on a playing card. The next deal, his opponent, Bonnie Jennie (Chaska, MN) was pegging her hand, and after playing three cards, discovered the 4th card was stuck to another card with Bob's chewing gum! A judge was summoned and her hand was declared dead.

A rumor circulated in the halls had it that the BOD may take another vote on his All-American honors at the upcoming BOD meeting in Raleigh! But, then again, anyone who would deal 29-hands to his opponents can't be all bad!

## Kah-Nee-Ta Medicine Men Put "Sign" On Cribbage Players

The confederated tribes put the "pox" on the cribbage games at the Kah-Nee-Ta Open in Warm Springs, OR. Many strange happenings were reported. Among them: Jeanne Hofbauer vs. Mickey Griffin, 1st hand: 4-4-4-4 on the peg, 2nd hand: 4-4-4-4 on the peg, 3rd hand, Mickey leads from a pair of fours, Jeanne has a four, but says, "Oh, no you don't...not again! Another game: R. T. Connely's first crib: four 4's. The second crib: four kings.

Then the playoffs: Bob St. Ives vs. Liz Brandon. Both players leave their game momentarily for coffee, and upon returning, no cards! After another game, they both leave again, and upon returning, no cards again! They finish their match without leaving their chairs again!

The winner of the tournament had room 13...and had game after game "donated" through strange plays.

The only explanation is the tribal medicine men were up to no good.

131

# $800 Up In Smoke!

At the recent Washington State meet, the doubles event players were in the process of tallying their final game. Tom Markham , Mt. Lake Terrace, WA, had his card tallied and slipped it under an ash tray momentarily. He was happily talking to his partner, Gary Bugg, Edmonds, WA, about their fine card and surmising about how much a 19 GP, 9-wins+132 card should win in a 10-game match.

Poof! Suddenly the score card under the ash tray burst into flames (see inset). Every score was burned beyond recognition. In horror, Tom took the remains to tournament director Willie Evans, asking for help.

With a twinkle in his eye, Willie says "tough luck...this card is forfeited!" After a few moments, letting Tom and Gary suffer a bit, Willie relented and with other player's help, they reconstructed this $800 card!

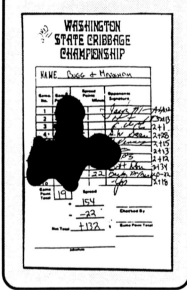

## What's Bob Brumley's Secret?

Bob Brumley, Sunnyside, WA has been burning up the track this cribbage year, scoring some 600 plus MRP's.

Bob is a 6' 3" 370 lb. hunk of muscle, complete with a fiery red beard. Could his secret to success be spelled I-N-T-I-M-I-D-A-T-I-O-N?

...and an ivory cribbage board... tournament style!

# Vignettes From Reno

With the record 736 players attending the ACC Open, there had to be a few unusual happenings...and there was.

For example, Joan Rein, secretary and BOD member of the ACC has been trying to score 7 MRP's for some time to earn her Master Rating. Alas, she scored only SIX...and remains at 1,999.

And how about Vern Ward, the Crescent City, CA flash...four chances at that elusive 29-hand. No luck.

Mickey Griffin, Lincoln, NE, buys his consolation card, goes to his room, flushes his toilet, and is shocked to see his card starting to go down the drain. Fast action saved his card, and with some toweling, and drying on his register, salvaged the card. Alas, he should have let it go...he failed to qualify.

Wayne Momsen, Butte, MT, scored that 29-hand...but in the Tournament of Champions. This event is NOT sanctioned, so no $100 ACC bonus.

# Unbeatable Pegging Mark Set in Nyssa, Oregon

In the small farming town of Nyssa, Oregon, on the banks of the Snake River, a pegging mark was set May 20, 1990 that is unbeatable!

Michelle Park, Buhl, Idaho, dealt Betty Capper, Hermiston, OR, four dueces...and she dealt herself four aces. The pegging was as follows: 2-3-5-6-8-9-11-12...and a "go" for a single point for Michelle. The final total of 12 will stand unchallenged (without a misplayed crib discard) hereafter (but perhaps tied).

However, wouldn't this have been much more exciting if these two players held 1-1-2-2 each? Then the final pegging score would probably be 29 to 12 in favor of the dealer.

# The Old College Try

One of the many stories that made it to your editor concerning play at the huge ACC Open in Reno was one concerning Jim McManus, Grand Master from Milwaukee.

Jim needed 50 points to win and was dealing. The situation looked impossible. His opponent was well within range to win on the next deal. Lo and behold, Jim's opponent scored a bad hand, while Jim nailed a "barnburner." And all the pegging went his way, too! With first count on the next deal, McManus scored another "barnburner." And more pegs!

Alas, it was just another case of the "old college try" as Jim came up ONE POINT short!

There, there, dear... Jim McManus doesn't play in **ALL** the tournaments!

### Medeiros Has Cribbage Fever

We all love cribbage, but this special man in my life (Bill Medeiros, S. Easton, MA) wants to take the game to his grave!

As you can see by the picture, he has on his monument a royal flush, 2 sets of dice (showing 7's for craps) and, of course, a cribbage board.

You can see he is one of the most dedicated players around, Or could it be that he'll be looking for a 29-hand well after his immortal life on earth?

I'm not sure God plays cribbage (even though a lot of people call on him while playing). I'm not even sure the devil plays cribbage even though we sometimes say "What the hell is this hand?!" But let's just hope Bill Medeiros doesn't go by his already made and waiting head stone and see a couple of skunks resting and waiting for him! Ha ha!

We love ya Bill!

*Sharlene Szaban*
*Ludlow, MA*

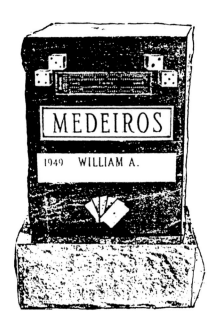

*PS: Head stone is located at Cambridge Cemetery, Cambridge, MA*

### Bill Medeiros' Head Stone Update

South Easton, MA pegger Bill Medeiros is rumored to have changed his headstone (see Nov. '91 CW). After finishing a lofty 2nd in the world's largest cribbage tournament, Cribbage World is predicting this stone now looks like this:

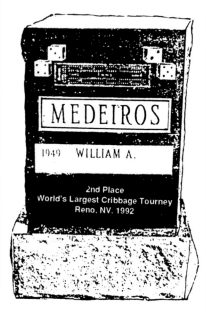

### Cribbage

With fifteen two, and eight are ten
upon a narrow board
Three centuries, and more, good men
their cribbage hands have scored.
And strangely, by the rules they made
three hundred years ago
The game today is being played
without a change to show.
What to throw the crib and what to hold
my father taught to me
"Turn me the jack, take two," he told
You get two points for every pair.
And so the game goes on
remember here and everywhere,
it's two for thirty-one.
Now this is what I would like to know
and often wish I knew
Who was it in the long ago
first counted fifteen two?"
My thought of cribbage as it's name,
the pairs and double runs
The pegs, the board, and left the game
for dads to teach their sons.

*Edgar A. Guest*

### What Next? Stadium Cribbage

Have you ever played Stadium Cribbage? Several years ago when my nephew attended college, he belonged to a fraternity that from time to time came up with very original ways of entertaining themselves.

One year about two hours before game time, two fraternity members solicited the help of four pledges and proceeded to play Stadium Cribbage.

The two players sat at a table on the football field's 50-yard line. The four pledges positioned themselves in the upper deck, two at the far left side of row five and two at the far left side of row ten. As play progressed, a megaphone was used to relay the number of seats ("holes") to be moved.

Play continued until the winning set of "pledges'" (pegs) reached the far right side of the upper deck. No one bothered to count off 121 seats. In some stadiums the game could easily go past 500 points. Has anyone else found other ways of playing?

*Dick Corbin*
*Raleigh, NC*

*In Ronan, Montana, the world's largest cribbage board...a behemoth 40 feet long by 8 feet wide (4 half slices of a huge cedar tree) was used in a game with the governor of Montana and the local champ. Two scantily -clad young ladies moved the 4-foot high pegs...and much fun was had by all. I forget who won the game...I was watching the "pegging action."*

*The editor*

### Cappers are Early Bird Players!

Ken and Betty Capper, the Hermiston, OR duo, were in Crescent City for the Bill Mitchell Memorial playing in the Friday Night Special. First Betty scored a 28-hand. A few minutes later, Ken plunked down a 29-hand...his lifetime 3rd! Alas, one day too early for the ACC's $100 for a sanctioned 29-hand.

Ken's 3rd ranks high among players, but who can top the unofficial 10 scored by Allan Lichty of Des Moines, Iowa? Cribbage World is standing by awaiting word of someone who has scored 11.

## The Game
by Bill Hyde, Sturgeon Bay, WI

*You can play just one on one*
*But three or four is more fun*
*Played for stakes and I have won*
*Played with wife just for fun*

*Fifteen two, fifteen four*
*Many times there is no more*
*Make a pair you take two*
*Form a run and peg a few*

*Nineteen hand may be your fate*
*Double run gets you eight*
*There are games and cards are punk*
*And are the victim of a skunk*

*Played all over with the best*
*Won a few and lost the rest*
*There are times you will cry*
*The cuts all go to the other guy*

*In position and hope to score*
*But deal your foe a twenty-four*
*Million games and I can whine*
*Never had a twenty-nine*

## Designated SNIVELING Area

# Vignettes "On the Trail..."

I have been "on the cribbage trail" for some 10 years, and it has been a most enjoyable experience. I have made hundreds of friends nationwide. Almost without exception, players have been great sports, win or lose. The camraderie among players is outstanding. I have participated in many sports, but the cribbage crowd stands alone as a "fun" group.

In these 10 years, admittedly "hooked" on cribbage, I have travelled some 200,000 miles pegging away with my friends and colleagues nationwide. And, of course, many unusual events have transpired over the years while "on the trail." I cannot resist spinning a few tales of humor, tragedy, exultation, and the unusual that I have experienced.

## Getting Hooked

I joined the American Cribbage Congress in 1981. In October of that year, I played my first sanctioned tournament in Wallace, Idaho. Forty-four serious peggers showed up to make a try at the "Idaho Championship."

My two young sons made the 120-mile trip over the mountains to Idaho, and when learning the championship came with a $500 prize, they cajoled me to buy two new bicycles if I should win. I agreed, as I really didn't expect to win. Lo and behold, my luck prevailed, and, indeed, I did win! My two sons sat behind me excitedly watching the final match. My match with Bob Anderson, a great sport from Wallace, went down to the final game. With the score 2-2 in the best 3 of 5 match, I ran a run of good cards to the championship. My two sons had a bicycle...and I was "hooked!"

## Trepidation in Las Vegas

With Winning this Idaho Championship...a sanctioned tournament...came an automatic invite to the American Cribbage Congress's Tournament of Champions, to be played in Las Vegas in December.

Another Montanan had also qualified. Gene Miller from Florence, Montana. Gene, Milo Roinstad (another serious pegger from my hometown), and I made plans to attend this meet, and the Las Vegas Open to be played the next day following the Tournament of Champions.

With a great deal of trepidation we headed south in Roinstad's old Buick. Gene brought his loyal, long white-haired (and very fat) dog along to make the trip. After a two-day, 960 miles trip, we arrived in Las Vegas, covered with dog hair. We nervously awaited the two matches...as this was the very first time we had played against the very best players in the nation. The National Champion (Norm Wright from Madison, WI) was on hand, and almost all of the ten All-American players from the preceeding year. What could three Montanans do competing with this crowd?

Gene did quite well, indeed, as he WON the Tournament of Champions! Wow! Gene bought Milo and I each a bottle of bourbon, and the best steak dinner in Las Vegas!

The next day we all played in the Las Vegas Open, and buoyed by Gene's win the previous day, I proceeded to win this event! Now we were truly an exuberant trio! With another steak dinner under our belts, we headed home. What a wonderful trip home! Two Montanans had taken on the best in the nation and come out winners!

We arrived home in great spirits...and covered with dog hair!

## Snowbound in Tremonton

Returning home from another trip south, Gene Miller, Milo Roinstad and I were caught in a severe snowstorm near the northern Utah border, and we were forced to "hole up" for the night in Tremonton, Utah.

With the wind howling, and the snow piling up, we found a motel behind a snow bank. Since it was Monday night, we decided to watch "Monday Night Football." I drove downtown and bought some hamburgers, being careful not to get stuck in the snowdrifts. Then, with a few before dinner drinks, and our hamburgers, we settled in to watch Dallas play Minnesota.

I placed a wager on Minnesota, and we were excitedly bantering about the game. In the third quarter, a Minnesota lineman came crashing in on Roger Staubach, the Dallas quarterback, and thumped him with a fore-arm on his shoulder pads. Staubach didn't go down from the thumping, and got the pass off. The referee threw a flag for roughing the passer! I let out a howl of protest, as this would certainly cost me my wager! Staubach wasn't even knocked down! How could he call roughing the passer? I continued my anguished howling...until a thumping on our motel wall! The patrons in the next room yelled at me through the wall...and I heard them loud and clear...to shut my big mouth!

We watched the game quietly from that point, and I paid my losing wager. The next day, the sun came out, and we continued home.

## $1.67 Speeding Ticket?

The next morning I began the drive from Tremonton to Montana. Since we had lost a lot of time due to the snowstorm, I was pushing the throttle down a bit...and I was pulled over near Dillon, Montana for speeding. We Montanan's are the last of the "liberal" states when it comes to speeding. The fine is only $5! At any rate, since I had lost my wager on the football game the night before, I demanded that Milo and Gene pay their share of the ticket...$1.67! And they did!

## In His Shorts?

The next year, Gene Miller, Milo Roinstad and I made a trip to Sparks, Nevada to play in the Tournament of Champions (moved from Las Vegas). The crowd was much larger in Sparks, and so was the prize money. Gene was on a roll...and he won the event again! A two-time winner in this very prestigious event. And he won a sizeable $1,500.

On the way home, we spent the night in a motel in the northern Nevada border town of McDermitt. The next morning, I jokingly asked Gene where he hid his money, as I couldn't find it after a search the night before. With a straight face he replied "I hid the money in my shorts!"

## My First All-American Award

All cribbage players in cribbageland covet an All-American award. The American Cribbage Congress awards the top ten finishers during a cribbage year (August 1 - July 31) All-American status.

During the 1985 year I was off and winging, scoring a sizeable amount of Master Rating Points early in the cribbage year. In late May, I decided to make a try for this honor and hit the road for Minneapolis, and the Minnesota Open.

Alas, I had a very poor tournament. The best I could do was pick up three measly Master Points. And I had driven some 2,400 miles! Did I feel like putting my head in a bucket of water, or what?

I was kicking myself over that trip...until the final results for the 1985 year were published. I had finished 10th with 443 MRP's! The number 11 player was Ray Boesel, from Glenbeulah, WI...and he had scored 442 MRP's. The trip to Minneapolis (and the **THREE** Master Points) had earned me my first All-American award! Of course, Ray Boesel wishes I had stayed home!

# Another One?

When the American Cribbage Congress switched their large Tournament of Champions, ACC Open matches to Reno, Nevada, along with two other events in Reno during the year, McDermitt, Nevada, became a regular stopping place for the night on our two-day journey to Reno.

McDermitt is a sleepy little town with one small casino ("Say When"). After stopping for the night on Thursday, Gene, Milo, and I walked across the street to play a little blackjack. We were the only customers on this weekday evening.

We began a conversation with the dealer about cribbage, about Reno, and the big tournament there, and so forth. Well, under my shirt, on a leather thong, I wear a silver hand (about half-life size) with a "29" in black letters on the palm. I asked the dealer if he had ever seen a "29-hand." He said no, so I exposed my "29-hand" from beneath my shirt and showed him a "29-hand." He got a big kick out of this and let out a laugh. The casino had one barmaid, who was leaning against the bar in a state of boredom (no customers). She sauntered over to look at the "29-hand" and said "How cute!"

The next Sunday, on the way home from Reno, we once again stopped at McDermitt for the night, and we once again played a little blackjack at the Say When casino. We had a new dealer, and since I had some fun with my silver hand on Thursday night, I repeated the same question: "Have you ever seen a "29-hand?" "No." And once again I brought my hand from beneath my shirt. The same barmaid was leaning against the bar. She came running over and exclaimed "My God! There was a fellow in here the other night with one of those!" I'm still laughing over that one!

# More Fun With My Silver Hand

I have had a lot of fun with that silver "29-hand" under my shirt. One of my more memorable jokes played with the hand was in a game with Roberta Dyer, a steely-eyed player from central Oregon...and she took the game seriously!

In a consolation qualifying round, Roberta was seriously pegging away, and since my score card wasn't so hot, I was in a playful mood. I said to Roberta: "Roberta, I feel lucky...I'll bet I'll show you a "29-hand" on the next deal. Give me 100-1 for a dollar (my penny, her dollar)."

She eyed me carefully. What a stupid bet, she must have thought. A 216,580 to 1 chance for only 100-1! She warily accepted the bet and dealt the cards. I picked up my hand...and quickly whipped out my silver hand from beneath my shirt. "Roberta! Here is a "29-hand!" Pay me the dollar!"

She reared back in her chair in surprise. Then she clenched her fist and waved it near my nose. "You want a knuckle sandwich!" she exclaimed. Well, no, not really...and the game continued!

# Arguing: A Life-Saving Device

Milo knew that I loved to argue, and he used this knowledge to save his skin on many occasions. Driving home in the wee hours from a tournament, I would start to nod from exhaustion, and the car wouldn't stay between the lines. Milo would immediately begin an argument...preferably about politics, as he knew he could get my "goat" in a hurry. I am a liberal Democrat for the most part, and Milo is a conservative Republican. I think we are both still alive because of this difference.

# You Must Sleep With Rex?

In the summer of 1986, my Master Points were among the leaders and I had a chance to win my 2nd successive All-American award. The last tournament of the cribbage year was the Portland Open. If I could score a few Master Points, perhaps I could finish in the top ten nationally.

Some 153 peggers showed up from throughout the nation. One was Bob Julian, a fine pegger from Milwaukee. Bob pulled me aside and said: "Do you know that if you should win this tournament, you will be national champion for 1986." I never thought of that possibility, as I was simply trying to finish in the top ten.

I had travelled to Portland with Milo Roinstad and Rex Paddock, and we arrived late at the hotel playing site. Rooms were short, so we three rented the last room. Alas, only two beds...and no rollaways were available. We decided to play a round-robin cribbage match, with the winner (high card) sleeping alone, with the two losers sharing a bed. Luck would have it, Milo won, and Rex and I had to share a bed.

And luck would have it that Rex and I both qualified for the playoffs the next day. Rex commented that wouldn't it be a rarity if we played for the title, as he was in the bottom bracket, and I was in the top. We could conceivably play the final match for the championship.

My cards have never been better! I rolled easily through my first six playoff matches...and I had arrived at the final match! A match, should I win, would give me the national title for 1986! Lo and behold, there was Rex as my opponent! What a shock! One of my best friends! I told Rex to play his very best...that I wouldn't have any hard feelings should he win.

My cards were still running hot. I won the match 3-0, with the last game being a real fluke. Only one card (of 13) on the cut would give me the third game, and, with the cribbage gods on my side, up came that one card!

What a wonderful trip home! And Rex had a new line with the ladies..."If you want to win the National Championship, sleep with me!"

# Did He See That Bottle?

My favorite travelling companion over the many years on the "cribbage trail" was Milo Roinstad. Milo was a retired machinist, rancher, tavern owner, and retailer. He was a very sociable fellow, and had a loud, infectious laughter...and he enjoyed life to the fullest. And he enjoyed a nip or two of his Ancient Age whiskey, too!

Milo really didn't enjoy driving, so I was the chauffeur, when I drove his car. This was a wonderful arrangement for Milo, as he could then have a nip or two from his leather flask that he stashed in the "jockey box" in the dashboard of the car. He would spin tales from the past, and we would argue on a variety of subjects, as we went merrily down the road.

One day, however, we were stopped at a roadblock on the Idaho, Oregon border. The Patrol was looking for an escapee. I was driving Milo's car, and the patrolman asked to see the car's registration. Milo opened his "jockey box" to get the registration, and his leather flask slipped out into sight.

The patrolman said, "Hey, mister, it's against the law in Oregon to have an open container in the car."

Milo replied: "Oh, okay, I didn't know that." And then he reached under the seat and pulled out a brand, spanking new bottle of Ancient Age whiskey.

I starting sinking down in the driver's seat. "Oh, no," I thought, "here we go with a big fine...or worse!" But, Milo has this cherubic look about him. His nose has a touch of pink, and he could pass for old St. Nick in a pinch...and after putting **BOTH** containers in the trunk, we were allowed to continue!

And to this day, Milo argues that the patrolman saw that bottle under the seat, and NOT the flask in the jockey box. We are both very argumentative types...and this story simply gave us one more topic "for discussion" as we travelled up and down the roads of the western United States.

# The Ten Cent Beer Can (or is it Five Cents?)

On one of our many sojurns to Reno, Milo and I had to travel through southern Oregon. This trip is a long, boring one, as the road stretches through miles of sage brush, with little else to see.

And to pass the time of day, Milo and I would trade yarns, but, more often than not, we would argue. The subject didn't matter all that much, we just loved to argue.

We had exhausted our supply of stories, and Milo idly said, "Look at all those beer cans in the ditch...did you know that in Oregon they are worth ten cents? The Oregon law makes a ten cent deposit mandatory on all drink containers."

"Ten cents!," I exclaimed! "That can't be right...it's too much!" And at every batch of beer cans I would argue that it just had to be too much...there were simply too many dimes laying around on the ground. But Milo stood his ground. Finally, I saw a bunch of cans on a bare spot off the road ahead, and said, "Enough of this, I'm stopping and we'll settle this, once and for all!"

I stopped the car, and we both got out to check beer cans for the amount of deposit stamped on the lid. We both had an empty, rusty can in our hands, checking the stamping, when two cribbage players from Pasco, WA (friends of ours) came roaring by, blowing their horn.

Wow! What an embarrassment! And sure enough, when we got to Reno, the two Pasco peggers gave us the raspberry. "What's the matter...you need gas money?"

Incidentally, I won the argument! The deposit in Oregon is FIVE CENTS per can! (And Milo and I even argue about who wins the most arguments!)

# California Championship!

October 20, 1984! Milo Roinstad and I made plans to attend the 3rd Annual California Championship in San Jose. I was to meet Milo in Carson City, NV, as he would be there on a gambling flight from Montana. We would then drive over the mountains to San Jose and do a little pegging.

Luck would have it that a severe snow storm had hit the mountains west of Carson City. At least all the television weather reports reported road closures, and impossible travel. With some trepidation, we set out for California, despite the weather reports. And, as is so often the case, the media made a mountain (of snow) out of a mole hill. The roads were clear, and the sky sunny and bright!

We arrived in San Jose without problems. The next morning we began play at Harry's Hofbrau House for the California Championship. I faired poorly in the qualifying round, but Milo had qualified for the play-offs. Milo began playoff play and I signed on for the consolation. I would get up from time to time from consolation play to see how Milo was doing in the playoffs. Even if I didn't get up to check, I knew he was still winning, as I could hear his laughter across the room.

After a time I looked up and they had Milo and a California player roped off for the final playoff! Wow! Milo had made the finals! He had been nipping a little at his Ancient Age whiskey, and he was in rare form. He was on a hot streak and was thoroughly enjoying it. Dick Cornwell, co-director of this meet, sat himself at the head of the table to watch play, and make judgements, if necessary. Milo was on a tear. I watched in amazement as he drew hand after hand. "24," "16,", "18," "20," "14," he would call. He never missed a hand in the best three of five match. Dick sat and watched and slowly shook his head, and smiled in resignation. His Californian was meeting his "Waterloo" at the hands of the Montanan. Milo won in three straight games. And all the games were easy skunks! What a wipeout!

Needless to say, we had a pleasant trip home!

## The Ice Man Cometh

Milo and I decided to play in the Minnesota Open in September, 1986. We had a most enjoyable trip, but we did not have an exceptional tournament (the Midwest is simply not my "stomping ground"...perhaps the players are wise to my style). However, we renewed many of our acquaintances with our fellow players from the Central Region.

It was a long trip home. Minneapolis is some 1,200 miles from our Missoula, MT hometown, and we drove 700 of them on Monday following the tournament. After a long-day's drive we decided to pull off for the night at Livingston, Montana.

Livingston is an old, sleepy railroad town, and has been in somewhat of a decline ever since Interstate 90 was opened and bypassed the town. The town has a couple of motels, but I spotted an old hotel. Across the street was the old railway station, and the old railroad repair shops were close by. "Milo," I said, "let's try that old hotel...that style of lodging is almost a relic. I'll bet it'll be fun to stay there." Milo readily agreed.

We entered the hotel to check in, and I immediately experienced a feeling of nostalgia. Ah, the good old days. The terrazzo floor, the potted palms, the solid oak registration desk, the ceiling fan...and, of course, the desk clerk with a green eye shade! I felt I was back at the turn of the century. The clerk (hotel owner, bell boy, manager, etc.) was a one-man show. We were the only customers in sight. After registering, he escorted us to the elevator. A rickety, steel cage, that clattered and clanged with every move. We slowly ascended to the third (and top) floor. After more clattering and clanging, the clerk showed us our room, and departed.

"Milo!" I exclaimed, "no TV! Now what are we going to do to spend the evening?"

"Geez," he retorted, I guess we'll settle in and swap some yarns. Let's have a before dinner drink, first!"

"Okay," I replied, " I'll go downstairs and get some ice."

I clattered and clanged my way down to the front desk, and asked the clerk for some ice.

"Ice? Ahh......, ice? I'm sorry, we don't have any ice."

I thanked him anyway, and walked a couple of blocks to a convenience store and bought a 5-pound sack of ice, and returned to our room. We proceeded to have our before dinner drink, and we were well into our repertoire of our past experiences. We were interrupted by the old elevator clattering and clanking. Then, we heard a strange scraping sound, and finally, a knock on the door.

It was the clerk. He was dragging a black plastic garbage sack half full of ice (about 40 pounds, or so). I was stunned, but thanked him profusely for his consideration. Wow! Enough ice for a month!

We swapped stories for a time, then walked down the street for dinner. After dinner, we decided to stop in and see what was going on at the local pub. Alas, Monday evening. No one was there, except the owner-bartender. We decided to have an after-dinner drink, and proceeded to swap stories with the bartender. Of course, the subject switched to cribbage right away...and Milo bragged about my exploits, and I bragged about his. Finally, the bartender had had enough!

"Hey, guys, how about one game each for $5?" We quickly agreed, as this would surely pay for half our room for the night.

You guessed it! He waxed us both, and we slinked home to our hotel room, $5 poorer. Upon entering the room, we discovered that we had an "ice-conditioned" room. Such is life in the fast lane!

## 121 Miles For A Game?

Every spring Milo and I would take off for Quincy, CA for their annual "World Championship." This one-day tournament sports a 14-game qualifying round.

On our third annual pilgrimage (a trip of some 1,700 miles roundtrip), I did a little arithmetic in my head.

"Milo!" I exclaimed, we are driving 121 miles for every single game of cribbage! Are we nuts...or what?"

Milo didn't answer...he just kept staring at the horizon miles ahead. To the left, and to the right...nothing but sagebrush! He didn't have to answer...I figured it out!

# Rex's 2nd 29!

The rarest cribbage happening I have seen is Rex Paddock's 2nd 29-hand. Let me explain.

Rex was pegging in the Capital City Classic in Helena, Montana, in September, 1986. In the qualifying round, he held an unusual hand...he was dealt 5-5-5-J-J-Q. The 5 of clubs was missing; the jacks were a club and a diamond, and the queen was a diamond. Rex, in haste, not wanting to throw matching suits to his opponent, discarded the jack of clubs and the queen of diamonds. Up pops the 5 of clubs for the starter card! Oops! This could have been a 29-hand! A rare 216,580 to 1 longshot. And $100 from the American Cribbage Congress for a sanctioned-event 29-hand! Needless to say, Rex was sick about his hasty play.

A month later, Rex is busily pegging away in the qualifying round of John Hill's Elbow Room Classic, a sanctioned event in Missoula, Montana. Unbelievably, Rex is dealt the exact same cards he misplayed in Helena! The 5-5-5-J-J-Q. Right down to the same suit! Precisely the same cards! Rex stopped play and announced to the crowd of peggers (and not even caring if his opponent knew what he was holding) "I'm not going to make this mistake again!" The crowd held their breath (as did Rex). Rex carefully cut the deck, and his opponent turned **THE FIVE OF CLUBS!** Astounding! The cribbage gods gave Rex a second chance...and he proudly claimed his $100, and a framed award from the American Cribbage Congress.

# Nice Guys Finish Last

In late January, 1985, I had qualified for the playoffs in the Western Open (later changed to the ACC Open) in Sparks, Nevada (played at Karl's Casino). I was playing in the 17-32 bracket, and with a win, would move into a much higher prize payoff...and more Master Rating Points.

My opponent was highly inebriated. Sloppy drunk is a more discriptive way to put it. We began play, and the third hand out he began pegging backwards. I pointed this out to him, and he said "I quit...I'm gonna' have another drink..." And he started to get up from the table. I hated to win this way...and I figured there was no way he could beat me...so I begged him to continue.

He reconsidered and sat down, and play continued. And the longer we played, the better he became. He began to sober up somewhat...and, needless to say, he won the match. My insistence that he continue cost me at least $200 and a pile of Master Points!

Nice guys finish last!

# Aren't You Glad Ray Won?

I have the dubious honor of playing in the final match with the oldest winner of a sanctioned event in the history of the American Cribbage Congress. Ray Rasmussen, Bend, OR., and I sat down to play for the Cascade Classic championship on June 22, 1986, in Redmond, OR. Ray was 82 years old at the time, and we had an exciting match. I recall the last hand vividly. I held a 2-3-3-10, needing but seven to win. An eight was cut, and I failed to peg a point! Ray nipped me 121-120! A stink-hole loss! I was crushed...as this was a very easy hand to help with the starter card, or at least peg one point. Second place was $550 less than first...making it a bitter pill to swallow.

Of course, Ray was elated! What a win! How exciting! Jeanne Hill, a fine pegger from Hermiston, OR, came up to me and said "Aren't you glad Ray won...he's such a fine gentleman?" I looked at her in amazement! I'm a fierce competitor...and I hate to lose! What could I say?

# A No-Win Situation

In the Oregon Championship in Prineville, OR in February 1987, I had qualified for the playoffs, and my first opponent was a young, 12-year old player. Ouch! A no-win situation!

Sure enough, the proud parents, and about 20 interested players gathered around to see if this youngster could wax the "old pro!" Either way, I was a cooked goose! But with valor being the better part of not losing, I squeeked by 3-2! The President of the American Cribbage Congress (a Grand Master, to boot!) got nailed this way one time. These kids have no respect!

# A Trained Bird?

In March of 1989, I was playing in Rob Palmer's Northwest Open in Baker City, Oregon. We had a sizeable crowd of 128 peggers on hand, and we were busily pegging in the qualifying round.

Rob opened the door on this nice, sunny spring day to let in a little fresh air. Shortly thereafter, a sparrow flew into the room via the opened door, and began frantically flying around the room looking for a way out. Meanwhile, I was engaged in a tough game with Jim Hartung. This Kennewick, WA player is a perennial winner at his club in Washington, and, with one hand to play, the outcome looked grim. All Jim needed to win was to hold me to less than 15 points and the game was his. My only chance, with first count, was a three of diamonds for the starter card, as I was holding an A-2-2-jack of diamonds. Lo and behold, up came the **three of diamonds!** And at that precise moment, the sparrow flew by and dumped a load of droppings full in Jim's face! Jim's first reaction was that a fellow player had thrown a grape, or whatever, at him. But once the hand was played out, he knew that luck was simply not in his favor that day!

Meanwhile, in the back of the room, Bo Van Orsow, a fine player from Redmond, OR, idly noted the bird flying around...and he swears he told his opponent "I'll bet that bird dumps on DeLynn's opponent...that's one of his tricks!" Believe it or not! (And we have 128 witnesses.)

# Riding With "Champs!"

Twice I hitched a ride to Raleigh, NC, to play in the National Open. In July, 1990, I made the long trek across country by joining Mickey Griffin (Lincoln, NE), Joan Rein (Chaska, MN), and Scott Kooistra (Yankton, SD), in the midwest for an all-night ride to Raleigh in Mickey's slick van. It was an enjoyable ride, and we had fun pegging away in the van...but we had even more fun on the way home! Scott Kooistra had topped the field of 434 peggers...and in the process had won the National Championship for the 1990 season! Wow! We were celebrating on the way home...and an even more enjoyable ride!

In the summer of 1992, I decided to try this method of getting to Raleigh once again. This time, Joan Rein had a new, slick van, and she invited me to join Scott Kooistra, Ron Morgan (Missoula, MT), and Larry Loupee (Newton, Iowa) for the all-night ride to Raleigh. We had another enjoyable trip. Time flew as we had our round-robin matches in the back of the van.

In Raleigh, however, it was Life Master Robert "Mick" Michaelis's (Marinette, WI) turn to win the National Open title. And in Raleigh, if you are playing the final matches in this double-elimination, best 4 of 7 match, you are still in town late Monday evening pegging away. Mick missed his flight home because of the playoffs, and he asked us if he could ride home in our van. Of course he could! Another enjoyable ride home! I'm batting two for two riding in vans across country! Twice I've ridden home with the champions of this prestigious tournament! I think I'll buy a van...maybe I could win one of those "Big ones!"

# The $2,000 Misplay

There is always the one bad play that really cost you the farm! Every player has them. My most serious mistake was in the "final four" playoffs in the Tournament of Champions on January 30, 1987, in Reno, Nevada. I was playing Mickey Griffin, Lincoln, NE, and we were tied 2-2 in the best 3 of 5 match. The winner goes on to the finals, and the loser plays for 3rd and 4th...and loses $2,000 in the process!

Mickey is dealing 28-points from home, and I am standing 22-points from home with first count. My strategy is to hold Mickey from scoring these 28-points in the next two deals (I cannot score the 22 points on my first count). I hold a poor J-7-A-A hand. I lead the jack, and Mickey plays an ace! I agonize over my next play. Do I play percentage and pair his ace, risking a 15-2 play or triples on the aces (I hold two of them)? Or play the 7 and perhaps get trapped with my aces. Dumb play! I pair the ace, and he triples up for **SIX big points**...and even though I come back with the 4th ace for 12 pegs, I cannot peg out to win the game. On the next deal, Mickey needs but 8, and gets them. Goodbye $2,000!

# Horrors!

June 19, 1988! Milo Roinstad, Gene Miler and myself travelled to Redmond, OR, to play in their annual Cascade Classic. 174 players were on hand, making this one of the largest tournaments in the northwest.

My cards have never been better! I was the top qualifier, winning 17 of 22 games. The added prize for this was a nifty $360 and a custom, hand-painted cribbage board, made by the famous board-maker Joe Nelson, Prineville, OR. The next day, my run of cards continued, winning 16 and losing only 7 in the playoffs. And in the final event, my match was with California's top player, All-American Butch Reynolds from Santa Maria. I won 4-2, with the key play being my 5-play on Reynold's 8 lead (I was holding 5-9-10-jack). He agitated and finally played a 9 for "22" and I played my 9 for "31" and 4 points! He was holding a 6-7-8-9. From that point on the match was mine. The prize was $1,500 and another large table model, hand-painted cribbage board! All in all, I had won $2,200.

Needless to say, I was on top of the world! Milo and Gene demanded dinner on the way home. I did not argue, and we stopped at a very nice seafood restaurant in Kennewick, WA. Price was no object! Gene and Milo ordered the largest lobster dinner on the menu. After stuffing on a fabulous salad bar, out came the huge lobster, complete with trimmings! We all stuffed on this fine meal, and headed for home...another five hours away.

We had been on the road no more than 10 minutes when Gene fell ill. He complained of a pain in his esophagus, caused by over-eating. We stopped at a truck stop on the edge of town, and he walked around for a bit...but told Milo and myself that this was not uncommon, he had this pain from time to time. Finally, he got back in the car, obviously not feeling well. I suggested we stop in Connell (some 25 miles down the road) for the night instead of driving home. Gene agreed.

About five miles from Connell, Gene slumped over in the back seat! Horrors! A heart attack! The time was 10:30 PM, and we were five miles from a small farming town! What to do? I stomped on the gas and flew into Connell. When we turned the corner into town, Gene sat up in the back seat, but immediately slumped over again. "Thank God!" I thought, he is still alive! Immediately I saw a police car two blocks ahead. Blowing my horn and flashing my lights got his attention and he stopped. I excitedly told him we have a heart attack victim in the car. He rushed to his car and radioed for medical help and he told me to follow him. A medical clinic was eight blocks away and when we arrived, I was amazed to see two medical technicians waiting! CPR was immediately applied in the parking lot. In five minutes, a doctor and a nurse arrived, and the clinic was opened. Gene was immediately given shots, electrical shocks, and other treatments. Alas, all to no avail...he had suffered a massive heart attack and passed away! Horrors!

From being on top of the world, I sank into a deep depression. This was the saddest day of my life! Gene was a wonderful person, and a great sport, win or lose. His untimely death will never be forgotten. I wish I had finished last and not made a dime...as the nurse said a large meal can trigger a heart attack...and if I had not won, Gene would have eaten a more modest meal and perhaps still be alive!

While making arrangements with the local mortuary, and answering questions with the police, Milo left to rent a motel room for the night. He came back with a key for room 13. And at midnight, when parking at the motel, a black cat ran in front of the car!

In retrospect, I have the greatest admiration for the medical staff in Connell. At 10:30 on Sunday evening, we received immediate, competent help. And Connell is a small farming town of less than 2,000! I gratefully tip my hat to the personnel who came to our aid that tragic night!

# Lucky Pennies

My superstitious nature has given me and my fellow players a lot of fun. I kill time around the tournament playing halls looking for "lucky pennies." And, of course, my competition knows this...and they play jokes on me.

Once I was asked to come out to the front steps to talk to someone. On the steps were hundreds of pennies strewn around! I had a good laugh, but objected to this method of finding a lucky penny. It HAS to be a random penny...and NOT salted!

Another time, we were driving Henry Popham's big white Lincoln...and we found a dozen pennies glued to the car!

And Ken Capper, a fun-loving pegger from Hermiston, OR, salted the parking lot, knowing full well I would be out looking. He laughed uproariously when I excitedly told him I had found a dozen lucky pennies!

Of course, since I have won more than my share at cribbage tournaments, my travelling companions do their share of looking for pennies, too. Once, we stopped for gas in Grangeville, Idaho, and while filling up the tank, the three other peggers were out scouring the driveway for pennies. Upon paying for the gas, the cashier said "What in the world are you guys looking for out there?" When I told her we were looking for lucky pennies she had a good laugh. But, on the way home, we stopped again for gas...and she excitedly asked how we fared at the tournament. She promised to "salt" a few pennies for us the next trip, since we didn't do too well.

After I won my seventh consecutive All-American award, you would be amazed at the number of players who have been spotted out looking for their "lucky penny!" Such is life on the cribbage trail!

# Never Brag!

After winning a national title, and a few All-American honors, you can get a little too cocky for your own good!

I was in good spirits playing in a qualifying round in Hermiston, OR...and I spotted a young chap down the line of players. I was due to play him next, and I whispered to my fellow players within earshot "Watch me intimidate this young kid!"

This kid...Matt Braukman...sat down to play, and I said "Hey kid, do you know that I won the national championship last year?" Mike didn't say a word...he just stared at me with steely black eyes, and slowly started unbuttoning his shirt. Then he quickly jerked open his shirt, and on his undershirt were the words "GOTCHA!" complete with a lightning bolt and garish colors!

This galvanized the players in our vicinity, and they all watched the game. It was a very close game from beginning to end, but this Hillsboro, OR kid did me in 121-119! Much to the delight of the players watching!

I learned my lesson then and there! NEVER BRAG! Cribbage is much too fickle to toy with! I have since learned that the Braukman clan has many expert players...and if you can come away with your shirt still on your back when you play one of them, you did quite well, indeed!

# An Invitation to Join the Gang "On the Trail"

I hope these vignettes about my many happy experiences "on the trail" will motivate you to join us for some pegging down the road. I invite you to join the American Cribbage Congress and join our fun-loving group! I want to sit down with you at our annual Awards Banquet at our yearly Grand National events, I want to play you for the $10,000 prize at our ACC Open, and I want to see you in Montana playing for our championship! Or peg for any championship nationwide! I guarantee, win or lose, you'll have a whale of a time pegging away! See you down the trail!!

# Appendix

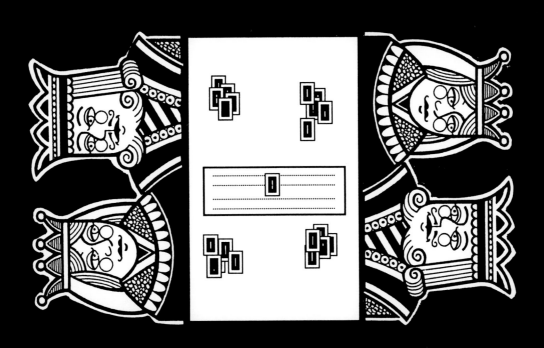

# Five-Card Cribbage
## (Sir John Suckling's Original Game)

Sir John's game was played with only five cards dealt to each player instead of the modern game's six-card deal.

The game is usually played to 61, with a lurch, or skunk, attained if a player fails to score at least 31. The game may also be played to 121 points (with a lurch attained if a player fails to score 91).

To begin play, each player cuts the deck. The player **cutting the high card** is the first hand's dealer. The non-dealer is entitled to immediately score three points to compensate for the advantage the deal gives the dealer. A peculiarity in the rules allows the non-dealer to score three points at any time during the game if he so chooses (except *after* his opponent has scored the winning point).

The dealer then deals five cards to his opponent and five to himself, alternating between the two and dealing one card at a time.

Each player discards two cards to form the dealer's crib. The non-dealer discards first.

The non-dealer then cuts the deck, and the dealer turns up the top card of the cut deck. This is the starter card and it scores the same as in six-card cribbage.

Pegging then begins with the non-dealer playing the first card. Pegging is scored in the same manner as six-card cribbage, except play stops at the first "go" or the first "31." If a player scores exactly "31" he scores two points. If play stops at a "go," the player playing the last card scores one point.

The crib has more importance in five-card cribbage than in the six-card variation. The crib contains five cards (including the starter card) while the hand contains only four cards (including the starter).

Flushes are scored as in six-card cribbage. The hand may score a three-card flush (all the cards in the hand are the same suit) or a four-card flush (the starter is also the same suit). The crib, however, must have all five cards of the same suit to score the flush bonus (five points).

Since the hand consists of only four cards, instead of five as in six-card cribbage, scoring is somewhat lower. Pegging to "31" only once keeps this aspect of scoring lower also. The averages every two deals are about 10 points less than the six-card game.

And despite Edmond Hoyle's criticism of six-card cribbage, the five-card variation eliminates much of the fun of pegging. The traps, the flush fakes, and, in general, much of the pegging strategy is simply not used when pegging up to "31" only once.

# Three-Player Cribbage

The rules of three-player cribbage are similar to two-player six-card cribbage.

Many cribbage boards have a third track to accomodate this game, but if your board has only two tracks, you may improvise by moving pegs side to side or track to track to avoid scoring conflicts. Each player has two pegs, preferably of different colors.

The game usually consists of 61 points, but players may agree to play 121.

The three players cut the deck. The player cutting the low card deals first. The deal then rotates clockwise.

The dealer deals five cards to each player in a clockwise rotation, one at a time. After the 15 cards are dealt, the dealer deals a 16th card to himself. This card is the foundation of the crib (and is set aside without the dealer looking at the card). All players discard one card from their hand to form the four-card crib.

The player to the left of the dealer cuts the starter card. This player also begins the pegging.

After pegging (in the normal manner), the hands and crib are scored. The player to the left of the dealer scores first. The dealer scores his hand and crib last.

All three players are independent, and strategy usually involves two players balking the leader and trying to improve their positions.

The winner, of course, scores double...one from each of his opponents. A player will be even if he wins one of three games.

The hands and cribs will score about the same as two-player six card cribbage. Since you discard only one card to your own crib, it is somewhat more difficult to "salt." Sir Edmond Hoyle was somewhat critical of the game, saying, "Ordinarily it is a poor enough affair!"

# Cribbage Solitaire

Jake the Snake has taken a vacation to Hawaii, paid for by his cribbage winnings, and has left you in the lurch with "cribbage withdrawals." What do you do with the daily hour or so usually spent playing cribbage with Jake? Why play cribbage solitaire!

This game is simple, fast, and difficult to win...but it can be done.

Cribbage solitaire consists of six hands and six cribs. In addition, you peg your six hands.

To begin, deal two cards down to form part of your hand. Then one down to form part of the crib. Deal two more to your hand, one more to the crib, and finally two more to your hand (your hand now has six cards, and the crib has two).

Of the six cards, discard two to form a four-card crib. Then *turn the top card* of the deck for the starter card.

Now peg your four-card hand for maximum count. For example, you are holding a 5-10-10-jack. Play the 5 first, then a 10 for "15-2," another 10 for "25, a pair and a go." The remaining jack also scores a "go" for one point. Your peg totals six points.

After scoring the peg, count your hand, then the crib.

To begin the second deal, the first hand starter card becomes one of the six cards to form your hand. Again, deal the crib two cards. Repeat this process until you complete the game with the sixth deal (the deck will contain four cards after six deals).

If you have played astutely and have had some luck, you can beat old man Solitaire, but it won't be easy. You must average 20 points per deal (plus one) to win this 121-point game.

This game doesn't tax the mind too much and should hold you until Jake returns from Hawaii, all tanned and raring to go!

# Four-Player Cribbage (Doubles)

In general, the rules for four-player (doubles) cribbage are the same as for two-player six-card cribbage. The game may be 61 or 121 points.

Play is by partnership. Partners are determined by cutting the deck, with two players cutting low being paired against the two players cuttng high. However, a team can be formed by mutual agreement (two friends, husband-wife, etc.)

Partners sit opposite each other. One player from each partnership is chosen to peg the score. Although his partner cannot touch the peg to score, he should carefully check for accuracy in pegging. Partners should also check each other's scoring of hands and crib to insure accuracy. Once an announced score has been pegged, it is too late to add additional points (however, you may correct backwards in the event of an over-peg with no penalty if your opponent's DO NOT catch the mistake. If they catch the mistake FIRST, however, the amount of overpeg is the amount of penalty).

One player from each partnership cuts for deal. The low cut wins the first deal (option: all four players cut for deal, low deals. One low tie, all tie, re-cut). The winners of the first deal specify which team member begins the game.

The dealer shuffles the pack and the player *to the right* of the dealer cuts the deck (an unusual rule). The dealer then deals one card at a time, beginning with the player *to his left,* until all players have five cards.

Each player discards one card to the dealer to form the crib. Of course, you discard to form a strong crib if it is your crib or your partner's crib, and discard balking cards to your opponent's crib.

The player *to the dealer's left* then cuts the deck and the dealer turns up the starter card in the same manner as in two-player six-card cribbage.

The player to the dealer's left plays the first card. Pegging is scored in the same manner as for two-player cribbage. Extra care must be taken in scoring as 16 cards are played and scored instead of eight. Care must be taken to insure that a "go" is completely played out. For example, a player plays a 2 for "29," and the other three players announce "go." The player playing the first 2 then may play a second 2 for "31" and score four points.

After pegging, the player to the dealer's left scores his hand, and scoring continues clockwise around the table. The dealer counts his hand and crib last.

Pegging assumes more importance than in two-player cribbage, as twice as many cards are counted, scoring more points as a consequence.

Scoring an extra hand and with the additional peg points, the averages every two deals are about 43 points vs. 26 for the two-player game.

# Six-Player Cribbage

A variation of the four-player game is played with three sets of partners, The rules and procedures are the same as four-player cribbage with the exception of dealing and seating.

Partners sit apart, separated by opposing players on the left and right.

The dealer's deals five cards to four players and *only four cards to the player to his right and to himself.* The four players to his left discard one card to form his crib.

Play continues in the same manner as in four-player cribbage. Care must be taken in scoring the pegs and hands, since so many cards are involved.

# Captain (3-player variation)

An interesting variation of three-player cribbage is "Captain."

The captain plays against the other two players and his game is 61 points, while his two opposing players play as a team and their game is 121 points. A skunk for the captain is scoring 45 points (or less) and a skunk for the other two-player team is scoring 90 points (or less). See diagram to the right.

All three players cut for deal. The player cutting the low card is "Captain." The next lowest card sits to the captain's left. The player cutting high card sits to the captain's right.

The captain deals five cards to each player in a clockwise manner, and deals one card to form the foundation for his crib (this card is not looked at, until the crib is counted, and is set aside). Each player discards one card to form the crib.

After all three players have discarded to the crib, the player to the captain's left cuts the deck for the starter card. Then the player to the left of the captain begins pegging, and play continues in a clockwise manner.

The player to the captain's left also scores his hand first, and the captain scores his hand and crib last.

This game is very popular in the midwest, especially in Wisconsin. The game is fast-paced, and an amusing variation of cribbage. Of course, a set is NOT complete until all three players have had a equal run at being captain. Many players prefer this variation of three-player cribbage to the more standard three-player game described earlier.

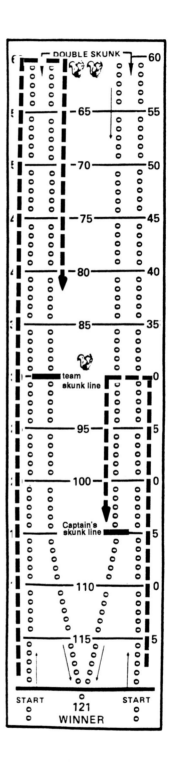

# CONSOLATION

0—Loss, 2—Win, 3—Skunk Win,

| GAME | 0-2-3- GAME POINTS | WIN + POINTS | LOSS — POINTS | Opponent's Initial |
|------|------|------|------|------|
| **Player's name** | | | | |
| 1 | | | | |
| 2 | | | | |
| 3 | | | | |
| 4 | | | | |
| 5 | | | | |
| 6 | | | | |
| 7 | | | | |
| 8 | | | | |
| 9 | | | | |
| TOTALS | | | | |

Net Score (+ or —)
TIE BREAKER

---

9th game opponent's signature
(I have carefully checked card)

---

Player's signature
(I accept score recorded on this card)

NO SMOKING
in playing hall
Nearby smoking
area will be provided

# CLIP ART

**The last four pages (151, 152, 153, 154) of this book are copyright free.** If you wish to use these scorecards for your own cribbage tournaments, simply add your "logo," print at your local copy shop and you're in business! Keep pegging!

## CRIBBAGE CLUB

| Game | 0-2-3 GP's | WIN + | LOSS — | Running Talley + or - | Opponent's Signature |
|------|------|------|------|------|------|
| **Player's Name:** | | | | | |
| 1 | | | | | |
| 2 | | | | | |
| 3 | | | | | |
| 4 | | | | | |
| 5 | | | | | |
| 6 | | | | | |
| 7 | | | | | |
| TOTALS | | | | | Games Won |

**CRIBBAGE**

**CHAMPIONSHIP**

**CRIBBAGE**

**Cribbage**

# CRIBBAGE CLASSIC

(YOUR LOGO)

# CRIBBAGE
# CHAMPIONSHIP

Seat Number

**SCORING:**
0 - LOSS
2 - WIN
3 - SKUNK

**TIE BREAKERS:**
1 - GAME POINTS
2 - GAMES WON
3 - SPREAD POINTS
4 - + SPREAD POINTS

| GAME | 0-2-3 Game Points | WIN + points | LOSS − points | RUNNING TALLY Games Won | Game Points | Spread Points + or − | OPPONENT (print last name) | Seat Number |
| --- | --- | --- | --- | --- | --- | --- | --- | --- |
| 1 | | | | | | | | |
| 2 | | | | | | | | |
| 3 | | | | | | | | |
| 4 | | | | | | | | |
| 5 | | | | | | | | |
| 6 | | | | | | | | |
| 7 | | | | | | | | |
| 8 | | | | | | | | |
| 9 | | | | | | | | |
| 10 | | | | | | | | |
| 11 | | | | | | | | |
| 12 | | | | | | | | |
| 13 | | | | | | | | |
| 14 | | | | | | | | |
| 15 | | | | | | | | |
| 16 | | | | | | | | |
| 17 | | | | | | | | |
| 18 | | | | | | | | |
| 19 | | | | | | | | |
| 20 | | | | | | | | |
| 21 | | | | | | | | |
| 22 | | | | | | | | |
| TOTALS | | | | | | | | |

*I have carefully checked this score card and attest it is true and accurate:*

**PLAYER'S SIGNATURE**

152

(YOUR LOGO)

PLAYER's NAME

# CRIBBAGE CHAMPIONSHIP

## Special Event

Seat Number

**SCORING:**
0 - LOSS
2 - WIN
3 - SKUNK

**TIE BREAKERS:**
1 - GAME POINTS
2 - GAMES WON
3 - SPREAD POINTS
4 - + SPREAD POINTS

| GAME | 0-2-3 Game Points | WIN + points | LOSS − points | RUNNING TALLY | | | OPPONENT (print last name) | Seat Number |
|---|---|---|---|---|---|---|---|---|
| | | | | Game Points | Games Won | Spread Points + or − | | |
| 1 | | | | | | | | |
| 2 | | | | | | | | |
| 3 | | | | | | | | |
| 4 | | | | | | | | |
| 5 | | | | | | | | |
| 6 | | | | | | | | |
| 7 | | | | | | | | |
| 8 | | | | | | | | |
| 9 | | | | | | | | |
| TOTALS | | | | | | | | |

*I have carefully checked this score card and attest it is true and accurate:*

Do NOT write below this line _____

| Game Points | Games Won | Spread Points |
|---|---|---|

**PLAYER'S SIGNATURE**

| | Player's name | | | |
|---|---|---|---|---|
| GAME | 0-2-3-4 GAME POINTS | WIN + POINTS | LOSS − POINTS | Opponent's Initial |
| 1 | | | | |
| 2 | | | | |
| 3 | | | | |
| 4 | | | | |
| 5 | | | | |
| 6 | | | | |
| 7 | | | | |
| TOTALS | | | | |

Net Score (+ or −)
**TIE BREAKER**

# CRIBBAGE CLUB *Chapter*

CRIBBAGE CHAMPIONSHIP

153

# CRIBBAGE
# Classic

**SCORING:**
0 - LOSS
2 - WIN
3 - SKUNK

**TIE BREAKERS:**
1 - GAME POINTS
2 - GAMES WON
3 - SPREAD POINTS
4 - + SPREAD POINT

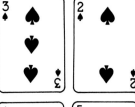

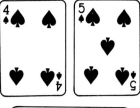

**RUNNING TALLY**

| GAME | 0-2-3 Game Points | WIN + points | LOSS — points | Game Points | Games Won | Spread Points + or − | OPPONENT (print last name) | Seat Number |
|---|---|---|---|---|---|---|---|---|
| 1 | | | | | | | | |
| 2 | | | | | | | | |
| 3 | | | | | | | | |
| 4 | | | | | | | | |
| 5 | | | | | | | | |
| 6 | | | | | | | | |
| 7 | | | | | | | | |
| 8 | | | | | | | | |
| 9 | | | | | | | | |
| 10 | | | | | | | | |
| 11 | | | | | | | | |
| 12 | | | | | | | | |
| 13 | | | | | | | | |
| 14 | | | | | | | | |
| 15 | | | | | | | | |
| 16 | | | | | | | | |
| **TOTALS** | | | | | | | | |

*I have carefully checked this score card and attest it is true and accurate:*

_____

**PLAYER'S SIGNATURE**

- - - - - - - - - - - - - - - - - - - - - - - - - - - - - - - -

☐ **$50 Friday Doubles (partner)**

☐ **$50 Friday High Roller**

☐ **$50 High Roller Q-pool (optional) (top 1/8)**

☐ **$40 Main Event (includes buffet lunch)**

☐ **$10 Main Event Q-pool (top 1/8)**

$_____ **Total    (Make checks payable to**

Name _____  ACC# _____

Address _____

City _____  State ____  Zip ____

The tournament Director reserves the right to refuse/eject any player any time for inappropriate behavior. I agree to abide by the rules of American Cribbage Congress and rules set by the Tournament Director

_____

Player's signature

154